Vintage Vibe
Quilts
& Projects

Vintage Vibe Quilts & Projects

Landauer Publishing, www.landauerpub.com, is an imprint of Fox Chapel Publishing Company, Inc.

Project Team
Acquisitions Editor: Amelia Johanson
Managing Editor: Gretchen Bacon
Editor: Amy Deputato
Copy Editor: Sherry Vitolo
Designer: Wendy Reynolds
Indexer: Jay Kreider

The following images are from www.Shutterstock.com: 12 pencil: Olga Kovalenko; 12 marker: BonD80;13 thimble: NataLT

ISBN 978-1-63981-067-3
Library of Congress Control Number: 2024941697

To learn more about the other great books from Fox Chapel Publishing, or to find a retailer near you, call toll-free 800-457-9112, send mail to 903 Square Street, Mount Joy, PA 17552, or visit us at www.FoxChapelPublishing.com.

We are always looking for talented authors. To submit an idea, please send a brief inquiry to acquisitions@foxchapelpublishing.com.

Printed in China
First printing

Vintage Vibe Quilts & Projects

CLASSIC DESIGNS FOR PRETTY, USEFUL THINGS

Louise Papas

Landauer Publishing

Contents

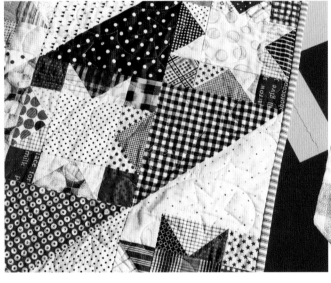

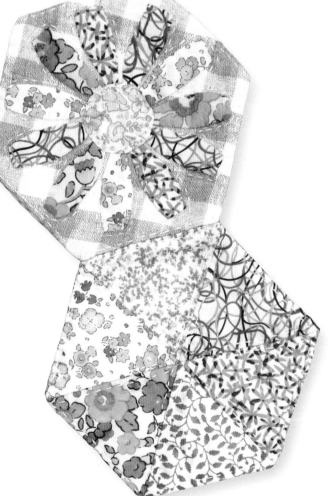

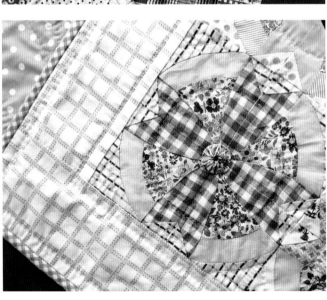

Vintage Vibe and Modern Style

A friend once described my quilting style as "vintage with a contemporary twist," and try as I might, I have never been able to make my quilts look modern. Each project in this book features vintage elements, from fabric to construction, and are contemporary interpretations of the beautiful old quilts I love. The projects use techniques like hand piecing and quilting, needle-turn appliqué, and paper piecing. Each piece will add a touch of vintage charm to your home and make a new special family heirloom.

My inspiration has come from many eras of quilting history and tradition. My favorite quilts are the lovely, scrappy, colorful American quilts made between the 1920s and 1950s (with a little bit of mid-century retro style from the '60s and '70s thrown in). I know I'm not alone in this passion, as I see many of these quilts being bought for large sums or rescued from estate sales and flea markets. They are all used, lovingly restored, or repurposed. For me, they continue to provide

inspiration for my own quilt designs as I find ways to meld old and new, whether it's the print or colors of the fabrics, a twist on a quilt design or quilting techniques, or a combination of all those elements.

USING VINTAGE QUILT DESIGNS

The 1930s through the 1950s was a busy time in quilt making. As well as being made for practical use, quilts were now being made for pure enjoyment of the craft and community activities like exhibiting at fairs. Block patterns were regularly appearing in women's magazines and national newspapers in response to growing demand. Popular designs included Grandmother's Fan, Flower Garden, Double Wedding Ring, Sunbonnet Sue, string quilts, yo-yo quilts, sampler quilts featuring a number of pieced blocks, and beautiful floral appliqué quilts. Many of these used small multicolored scraps left over from garment

Vintage style is timeless and it's easier than ever to research different design and construction techniques from the past.

making and other sewing projects, but they also made use of precut project-specific scrap-fabric packs.

We now have dozens of resources available to us for inspiration, including social media, websites, blogs, and books that share photos and information on the history of quilt making, allowing us to easily incorporate these old ideas into new quilts.

MIXING VINTAGE AND MODERN FABRICS

I have never used a complete fabric range in a single quilt and much prefer a scrappy mix of color, style, and pattern to emulate the early- to mid-20th century quilts I love. Using a fully coordinating range of fabric would take the fun out of quilt making for me, as choosing the fabric is an important part of my design process. I generally buy smaller cuts of fat sixteenths, fat eighths, fat quarters, or at the most a quarter to half a yard. This also allows me to have a broad range of fabrics in my stash to choose from. I use a variety of amazing designs from modern fabric designers, but I am also always looking for ways to add that vintage feeling through fabric.

To easily inject vintage style into your quilting project, many manufacturers offer reproduction fabrics that recreate the patterns and colors from a particular period. Earlier ones from around 1775–1825 include toiles, chinoiserie, and more European-style florals, while Civil War-era fabrics from 1850–1880 feature smaller patterns like paisleys, stripes, and florals in muted reds, browns, greens, and mauves. Then there's

Combining unexpected fabrics can often make a quilt sing.

my favorites, the fun 1930s–1950s fabrics that were bright and fun pastel tones, including solids and highly collectible printed feedsacks. You can also find reproductions of the more recent but still retro bright floral and graphic patterns of the 1960s and '70s.

One of my favorite features of old quilts is the repurposing of old clothing, curtains, sheets, and other household items. Old linens, including embroidered pieces, cotton shirting, and bark cloth are all wonderful options for introducing a vintage feel to your project. The different textures can be used together to create a really scrappy look and feel. Consider shopping at your local thrift store, flea markets, estate sales, or online to find some older gems.

Over the years I have collected bits and pieces of fabric of all types, including some special fabrics from my childhood. All have provided inspiration for my designs and more often than not, I only need a single fabric to take me on a whole new design journey.

THE TIMELESSNESS OF PATTERN AND COLOR

Sometimes you want a softer look to reproduce the look of a worn and faded old quilt. Or you might want to capture the fresh, bright florals of a 1930s scrappy quilt and mixing in some fun novelty prints with fruits, kitchen items, or animals will replicate the "use what you have" look of the Depression era. The use of bold graphic prints and geometric patterns with their lovely angles adds wonderful movement and timeless interest to a quilt.

My favorite vintage quilts are not symmetrical or square and often have a clashing color palette. You can easily recreate this look by avoiding placing your directional fabrics in the same way and by playing with pattern scale. If you don't think you have enough of one fabric, use it anyway and add something similar once you run out. Patching fabrics together to cut out block pieces was quite common in the past and can help stretch your favorite fabrics a bit farther. Combine things you would never normally put together or add a fabric you really don't like—these unexpected pieces can often make a scrappy quilt sing!

Include color combinations like the gorgeous pink and green pastel tones of the 1930s or the rich browns and oranges of the 1960s and '70s. Use off-white or cream for backgrounds instead of white to give your quilt an aged quality. Many modern quilters love a "low-volume" scrappy background that includes subtle patterns that read as one, allowing strong contrast against the brighter feature fabrics. Mixing colors and patterns will give your quilt texture and character.

Print, pattern, and color all have quite an impact in any quilt and can definitely add some vintage style.

BLENDING OLD AND NEW CONSTRUCTION TECHNIQUES

Although there were sewing machines available, many of the early-20th century quilts were made by hand. I mostly hand piece as I enjoy it and find it to be more accurate and flexible. I also don't have a dedicated sewing space so I like that I can do it anywhere. I also love the feel of the finished quilt and the process. Some of my favorite quilts of the 1930s were hand quilted simply with an all-over quilt pattern like the Baptist Fan, echo quilting, or cross hatching. Many were simply tied together. I love using thicker perle cotton thread to hand quilt (often referred to as "big stitch" or "utility" quilting) as it is a faster process than traditional hand quilting and allows for the addition of a beautiful range of thread colors.

Finally, how you finish the edges of a quilt can also add a special vintage element to the whole design. Shaped edges, in which the binding followed the block design, or curved corners were quite popular. These would have been bound with a single-fold bias binding to bend around the curves. Some quilts were finished with prairie points that were added to the quilt edge without using any binding. Other quilts used a simple facing stitched to the back and many were just bound with straight edges without the mitered corners we see most commonly today. No matter which vintage elements you mix and match, I hope you love the vintage-inspired design process as much as I do!

Using hand quilting and ties together in a quilt can add a lovely vintage touch and gives a beautiful, soft, and textured finish.

Some quilts were finished with prairie points added to the quilt edge without using any binding.

Getting Started

Before you begin, there are a number of skills and techniques that will help you tackle the projects in this book. Preparation and a little bit of practice can make all the difference to successfully completing your project.

Choosing Fabrics

When choosing fabrics for a project, consider your overall theme or look. Do you want a scrappy vintage look or a more controlled color palette? A simple way to start is to choose one main fabric, then add coordinating and complementary fabrics. For example, you could start with a multicolored floral and then choose colors from within the fabric pattern to build your palette. For a great scrappy look try to include a variety of small- and large-scale patterns, including florals; geometric patterns like checks, spots, and stripes; and designs that provide movement to create interest. If you are unsure of where to start, always ask at your local quilt store—they will know their fabric range and what works well together.

A mix of small- and large-scale prints in a variety of colors will help create that classically vintage scrappy look.

Tools

You likely have most of the items you need in your sewing kit already, but there are some special pieces that will make the whole process smoother and more enjoyable.

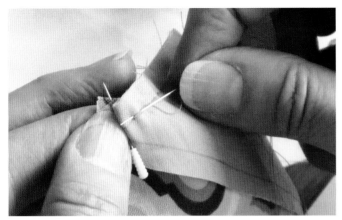

Needles—For hand piecing and needle-turn appliqué I like to use a fine needle, as it allows better control when you are sewing small pieces. I love milliner needles (also known as straw needles), and usually use size 10 or 11, which are the finest. Needles can have different eye shapes, which affects how easy they are to thread. I recommend trying a few so you can choose something that works for you. For hand quilting with perle/pearl cotton thread, I use a redwork/embroidery size 9 needle or a chenille needle, as they are sharp and easier to thread.

Thread—Use a good-quality 100% cotton thread for both hand and machine piecing. I prefer to use neutral colors like pale gray or green or creams and whites that disappear into the background. Try a few different threads, as you will probably develop your own preference. I use a 50-wt thread for hand and machine piecing and a finer 60- or 80-wt thread for appliqué.

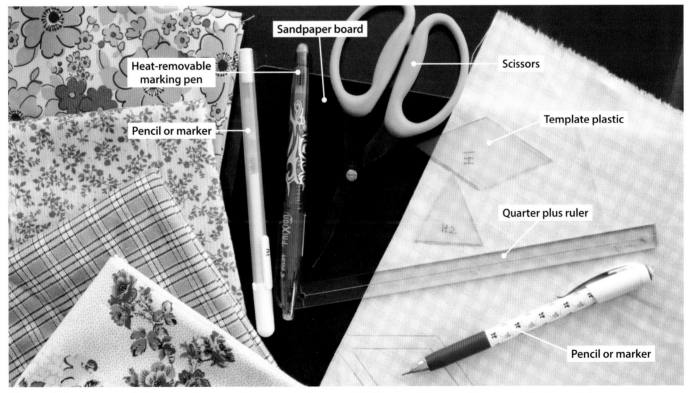

Sandpaper board

Heat-removable marking pen

Pencil or marker

Scissors

Template plastic

Quarter plus ruler

Pencil or marker

The tools here are useful for most types of sewing, but especially if you will be creating and using templates.

Pencil or Marker—To trace around your templates on your fabric, you need a fine lead pencil or gel marker. For lighter fabrics, you can use a mechanical pencil with a 2B 0.07 lead or a ceramic lead pencil. The ceramic lead is a bit tougher and less likely to snap in an acrylic template. For darker fabrics, a fine silver or white gel marker will show up well.

Heat-Removable Marking Pen—These are great for tracing around appliqué shapes. The line will be turned under as you sew, but any residual marks can be removed by holding the iron above them. I don't recommend these on fabric for any other uses as the lines can return in the cold and leave silvery shadows.

Scissors—Always use good-quality scissors as they will last you longer. For hand cutting, I prefer a smaller pair of scissors, which provides greater control and accuracy when cutting small pieces. I use Karen Kay Buckley Perfect 6" scissors most often—they have a serrated blade to grip the fabric and prevent slipping. Thread snips are also very useful whether you are machine or hand piecing. They are quick and convenient and can get in nice and close to your fabric to snip threads without damaging your project. I also like to keep a pair of paper scissors handy for cutting plastic templates.

Quarter Plus Ruler—These are used to mark your seam allowance once you have traced around your templates. There are several different versions available.

Template Plastic—This is a lightweight, clear plastic used to make reusable templates. You can purchase plain or gridded varieties depending on your requirements. This material is great for fussy cutting as you can see through it for accurate fabric placement.

Permanent Markers—Using a fine permanent marker to trace your templates onto template plastic avoids smudging and provides a nice sharp line.

Sandpaper Board—Lay your fabric on a sandpaper board as you trace around your templates to avoid the piece shifting and distorting the drawn lines. You can buy them attached to a wooden board or in a folder that includes a cutting mat and padding to use as an ironing surface. You can also make your own using a fine-grade sandpaper sheet.

Pins—Fine patchwork pins work well for machine piecing. For hand piecing and appliqué, I like to use shorter appliqué pins as they don't get in the way on smaller pieces.

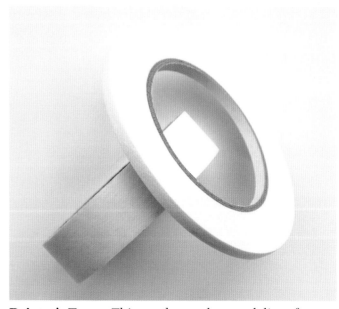

Painter's Tape—This can be used to mark lines for quilting. One piece can be lifted and moved several times but should not be left on your quilt for long periods. It is also useful for taping your quilt backing down during the basting process.

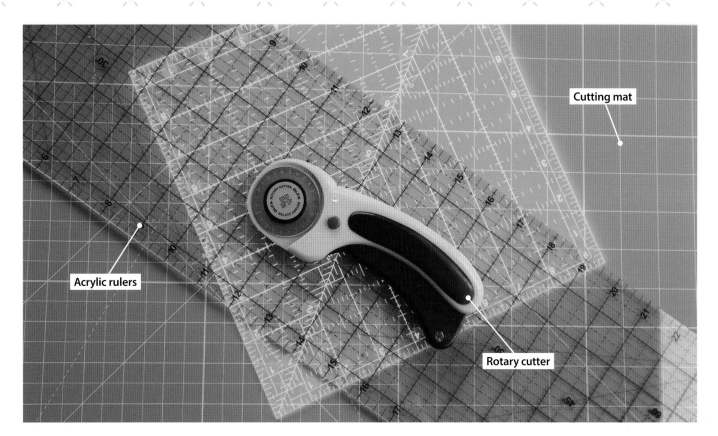

Cutting mat

Acrylic rulers

Rotary cutter

Rotary Cutter and Self-Healing Cutting Mat—
Cutters and mats both come in various sizes. A
45mm-blade rotary cutter and 18" x 24" (45.7 x 61cm)
cutting mat are the most commonly used sizes for quilt
making. Keep your rotary cutter blade locked when not
in use and always use a self-healing cutting mat to help
keep your blade from dulling quickly.

Acrylic Rulers—There are many shapes and sizes
used for cutting with your rotary cutter. I mostly use a
6½" x 24" (16.5 x 61cm) ruler.

Seam Ripper—We all make mistakes and it's
important to have a trusty seam ripper in your tool kit.
I use a Clover as it's nice and sharp and easy to hold.

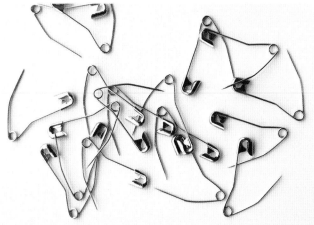

Curved Safety Pins—These are specifically designed
for the purpose of basting through the layers of a quilt.
I like to leave mine open in a box to save myself from
having to reopen them the next time I baste a quilt.

Thimble—There are many options
for protecting your fingers while
piecing and quilting. I prefer
leather thimbles since they are
protective and soft, but you can
try metal, plastic, or rubber
thimbles or even smaller plastic
or leather stickers depending
on where your pressure points
are and what feels comfortable
to you.

How to Make and Use Templates

To make your templates, use a fine permanent marker to trace the template shape onto the template plastic along the stitching line (the inside line). Cut out the template along the drawn line and label it with the template number. Try to draw as accurately as you can and cut exactly on the line, as this can affect the size of the finished shape and the accuracy of the finished quilt. **Note:** When a pattern mentions creating a template in reverse, you must flip the template over and trace as usual to get a mirror image of the shape.

To use patchwork templates for hand piecing, place your fabric right side down on a sandpaper board and, making sure you are straight with the grain of the fabric, trace around the edge of the template using your pencil. Then, using a quarter plus ruler, mark your seam allowance and cut out the fabric pieces with scissors. Try to be economical with your fabric by placing the templates in rows rather than randomly over the fabric. You may also want to "fussy cut" a particular part of your fabric to create the needed shape.

To use appliqué templates, place your fabric right side up on a sandpaper board and trace around the edge of the template using a heat-removable marking pen. Cut out the template using a generous ⅛" (3.2mm) seam allowance.

Rotary Cutting

Even with hand piecing, there are faster ways to cut larger pieces like sashing and borders. Rotary cutting is the best option in these cases. From rotary-cut strips, you can crosscut to create squares and rectangles.

Rotary cutting is the most efficient way to create multiple long strips of fabric.

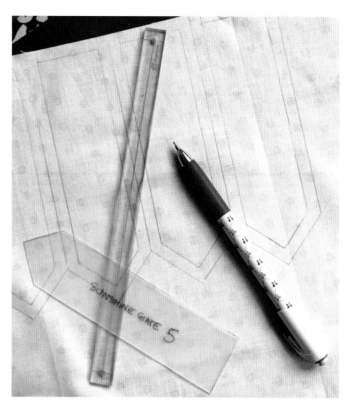

Be strategic in placing your templates to get the most out of each piece of fabric.

Once you gain confidence, you can even start to cut multiples by layering your fabrics.

Before any cutting can begin, however, the fabric needs to be squared up. Fold your fabric so the selvages line up. Place it on your cutting mat with the folded edge at the bottom and the selvages at the top. Line up your ruler so that a horizontal line on the ruler is in line with the folded edge and the vertical side of the ruler forms a right angle. Holding the ruler down firmly with your hand and keeping your fingers out of harm's way, press the rotary cutter down firmly and roll it away from you along the edge of the ruler, trimming away the edge. The fabric is now squared and ready to cut into strips.

Gently pick up the fabric and lay your cut edge down to the left, being careful not to mess up your nice straight edge. Place your ruler over the fabric with the desired measurement on your ruler at the cut edge. Always make sure you double check your required measurement and that you have the ruler on that line. Check that your ruler is making the right angle by lining up the bottom edge with a horizontal line on your ruler. Press the rotary cutter down firmly and roll it away from you along the edge of the ruler. Cut strips by moving across the fabric and keeping an eye on your right angle.

You can remove the pins as you work. If you pin as I do, your last pin will be the first pin you placed in Step 1.

Hand Piecing

Many modern quilters are familiar with machine piecing, but hand piecing might be a bit unfamiliar. The steps are very straightforward.

1. Pin your pieces together, matching the marked lines on the front and back fabric. I like to start pinning at the end point and pin across to where I will start sewing.

2. Sew using a small running stitch along the seam line, adding a back stitch about every ½" (12.7mm). Finish with a back stitch and then knot the thread. When you cross seams, always make a backstitch just before you pass your needle through to the other side of the seam and then again on the other side of the seam. This makes the joins stronger and avoids leaving any gaps.

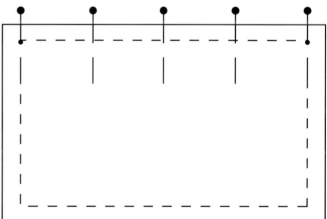

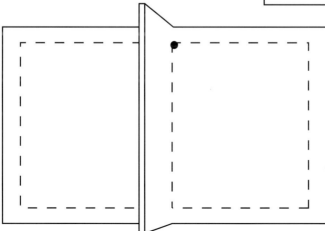

When hand piecing, you don't sew into the seam allowance, allowing you more flexibility with Y seams and around corners.

Use the templates for the projects to create pieces that fit together perfectly with the correct seam allowances.

Needle-Turn Appliqué

Needle-turn appliqué is the process of sewing a shape to a background by using the needle tip to turn under the fabric edge as you sew it down, leaving a nice, smooth edge and no visible stitches.

1. Trace around your template on the right side of the fabric and cut it out, adding between a ⅛"–¼" (3.2–6.4mm) seam allowance.

2. Pin or baste the pieces to your background using a light box or a window to help with placement. You can trace the appliqué image onto baking or tracing paper and lay it over the background to guide where your pieces will be positioned, or you can trace the image onto your background and stitch the pieces onto the image. Always look at your pattern to determine which pieces go first, as some will sit under others. You don't need to needle-turn parts that are covered, but you can baste them down as you are appliquéing the rest of the shape to keep them flat.

3. Finger press under the edge of the piece along a straight section to get things started before you come to any points or inside curves.

4. Using a knotted fine-weight cotton thread, bring your needle up through the background and then use the needle tip to turn under the fabric along the drawn line as you stitch. You will turn under about ½" (12.7mm) of the edge ahead of stitching as you go and hold it in place using the thumb of your other hand.

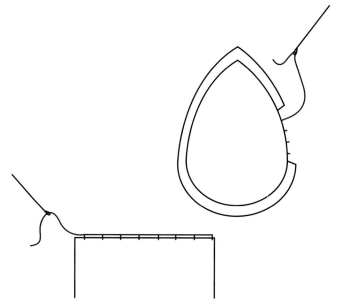

5. Stitch directly into the background close to the turned edge and move along underneath about ⅛" (3.2mm). Bring your needle back up and stitch very closely through the appliqué piece's turned edge.

6. Repeat, making sure you go back into the background close to the turned edge and exactly where you came up. If you go slightly to either side, it will create a small visible stitch, which you want to avoid.

When stitching a point, sew up to the point and make another stitch right on the point to secure it. Then turn your work and, using your needle, fold the corner under to the left to tuck it in. Continue to needle-turn and stitch along the line.

If you are stitching an inside point or an inside curve, you need to clip into the seam allowance close to the drawn line.

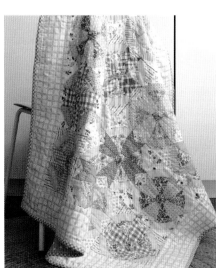

The Quilts

Read all of the instructions before you begin. It helps to have an idea of how the project flows and what you will be doing before you start. Press all of your fabrics as they will be easier to rotary cut and easier to trace templates onto. Check that your fabrics are colorfast. If some will bleed, wash all of them. I generally don't wash my fabrics before I start a project.

Clinker

Quilts were often tied as an alternative to quilting to provide quick, easy, and warm bed covers for the home. Tied quilts are still popular and are thought to hold heat better than their quilted cousins because of the larger air pockets between the ties. They also have a wonderful homey finish. This simple brick wall design is rotary cut, machine pieced, and then tied with perle cotton thread—so it's super fast to make. I have used a cotton batting, which feels soft and drapey, but you could use a higher loft batting to give your quilt a puffier finish.

FINISHED QUILT SIZE: 72" x 60" (183 x 152.5cm)

REQUIREMENTS

- Fat sixteenth of each fabric for colors 1 and 19
- Fat quarter of each fabric for colors 2, 3, 4, 5, 15, 16, 17, and 18
- ⅜ yd. (34.3cm) of each fabric for colors 6, 7, 8, 9, 10, 11, 12, 13, and 14
- 3⅝ yds. (3.3m) backing fabric
- 76" x 64" (1.9 x 1.6m) rectangle batting
- ½ yd. (45.7cm) binding fabric
- Rotary cutter
- Ruler
- Cutting mat
- Coordinating cotton thread
- Embroidery needle
- Size 8 perle cotton thread

CUTTING INSTRUCTIONS

- From colors 1 and 19, cut:
  - One 6½" x 4½" (16.5 x 11.4cm) rectangle
  - One 3½" x 4½" (8.9 x 11.4cm) rectangle
- From colors 2 and 18, cut:
  - Three 6½" x 4½" (16.5 x 11.4cm) rectangles
  - One 3½" x 4½" (8.9 x 11.4cm) rectangle
- From colors 3 and 17, cut:
  - Five 6½" x 4½" (16.5 x 11.4cm) rectangles
  - One 3½" x 4½" (8.9 x 11.4cm) rectangle
- From colors 4 and 16, cut:
  - Seven 6½" x 4½" (16.5 x 11.4cm) rectangles
  - One 3½" x 4½" (8.9 x 11.4cm) rectangle
- From colors 5 and 15, cut:
  - Nine 6½" x 4½" (16.5 x 11.4cm) rectangles
  - One 3½" x 4½" (8.9 x 11.4cm) rectangle
- From colors 6 and 14, cut:
  - Eleven 6½" x 4½" (16.5 x 11.4cm) rectangles
  - One 3½" x 4½" (8.9 x 11.4cm) rectangle
- From colors 7 and 13, cut:
  - Thirteen 6½" x 4½" (16.5 x 11.4cm) rectangles
  - One 3½" x 4½" (8.9 x 11.4cm) rectangle
- From colors 8, 9, 10, 11, and 12, cut:
  - Fifteen 6½" x 4½" (16.5 x 11.4cm) rectangles
- From the binding fabric cut:
  - Seven 2¼" (5.7cm) x WOF strips

CONSTRUCTION

1. Construct the quilt in rows, starting from the bottom and finishing at the top. You will add a new fabric as a half block on the left of every second row. The Quilt Assembly Diagram is marked with the color numbers for each block in each row. Starting at the bottom right-hand corner with color 1, stitch together one block each of colors 1–12 to form row 1, as shown.

2. Continue to follow the Quilt Assembly Diagram, stitching together rows 2 through 15.

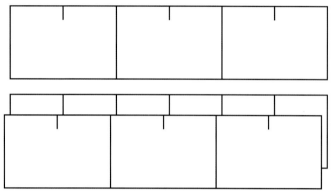

3. To make sure the rows line up properly, mark the 3" (7.6cm) point at the top of each full block with a pencil. Pin row 1 to row 2, matching the pencil mark on row 1 to the seam on row 2 as shown. Repeat to join the rest of the quilt.

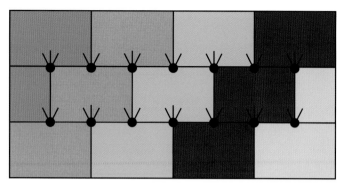

4. Baste the backing fabric, batting, and quilt top together. Thread the embroidery needle with a long double perle cotton thread. Insert the needle through the layers and come back up to the front ¼" (6.4mm) away from where you put the needle in, leaving a 2" (5.1cm) tail. Repeat this stitch, then tie a square (reef) knot—tying twice, right over left then left over right. Trim the threads to about ½" (1.3cm). Tie the quilt at every seam intersection as shown to create an even grid across the quilt.

5. Bind using the instructions in the Finishing Your Project section on page 107.

Quilt Assembly Diagram

This pattern builds up gradually row by row, making it an approachable but impressive project.

Fruit Cocktail

This pretty peach pastel background takes these simple scrappy blocks set on-point straight back to the popular bright and colorful quilts of the 1930s. This quilt is made using three blocks. Block One features an economy block center and Block Two features a four-patch. These are alternated with a background block. Bind it with a bold bias-cut plaid for a fun and unexpected finish!

FINISHED QUILT SIZE: 60" x 68" (152.5 x 172.7cm)
FINISHED BLOCK SIZE: 6" (15.2cm) square (6½" [16.5cm] square with seam allowance)

REQUIREMENTS

- 4 yds. (3.7m) assorted patterned fabrics for blocks 1 and 2, including stripes, spots, checks, and florals (fat sixteenths and fat eighths will work)
- ⅜ yd. (34.3cm) assorted solid color fabrics for centers of blocks 1 and 2
- 2 yds. (1.8m) peach background fabric
- One 68" x 76" (1.7 x 1.9m) rectangle batting
- One 68" x 76" (1.7 x 1.9m) rectangle backing fabric
- ⅜ yd. (34.3cm) plaid binding fabric
- Templates on pages 110–111
- Rotary cutter
- Ruler
- Cutting mat
- Coordinating cotton thread
- Template plastic
- Fine permanent marker

PREPARATION

Make the templates by tracing them onto the template plastic using a fine permanent marker. Cut them out on the line and label them with their numbers.

CUTTING INSTRUCTIONS

For Block One (28 blocks total)

- From the assorted patterned fabrics, cut:
  - Eight T1 pieces (224 total)
- From one of the patterned fabrics, cut:
  - Four T2 pieces (112 total)
- From another of the patterned fabrics, cut:
  - Two T3 pieces (56 total)
- From a solid color fabric, cut:
  - Two T3 pieces (56 total)

For Block Two (28 blocks total)

- From the assorted patterned fabrics, cut:
  - Eight T1 pieces (224 total)
- From one of the patterned fabrics, cut:
  - Four T2 pieces (112 total)
- From another of the patterned fabrics, cut:
  - Four T5 pieces (112 total)
- From a solid color fabric, cut:
  - One T4 piece (28 total)

- From the peach background fabric, cut :
  - Forty-two 6½" (16.5cm) squares
  - Twenty-six T6 setting triangles (make sure the long edge is on the straight grain)
  - Four T7 corner triangles (make sure a short edge is on the straight grain)
- From the binding fabric, cut:
  - The number of 2½" (6.4cm) strips needed to make up 8 yds. (7.3m) in length when joined end to end (*Refer to the bias binding cutting method under Binding on page 108.*)

MAKE BLOCK ONE

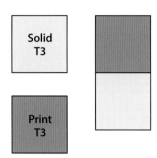

1. Pin and sew a solid color T3 piece to a print fabric T3 piece. Repeat. Stitch these two units together, making sure you alternate the colors.

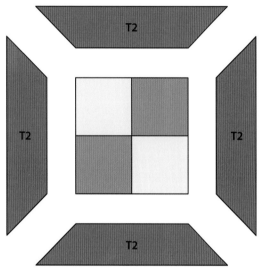

2. Pin and sew four T2 pieces to each side of the joined T3 unit and then stitch them together at the corners.

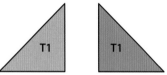

3. Pin and sew two T1 pieces along one short side. Repeat to make four.

4. Pin and sew a joined T1 unit to each T2 edge. Repeat to make 28.

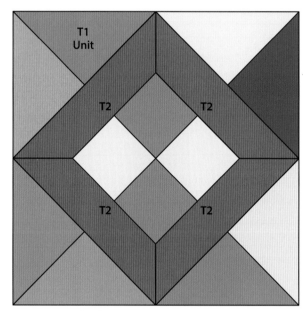

Block One Assembly Diagram

MAKE BLOCK TWO

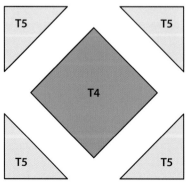

1. Pin and sew four T5 pieces to each side of a T4 piece.

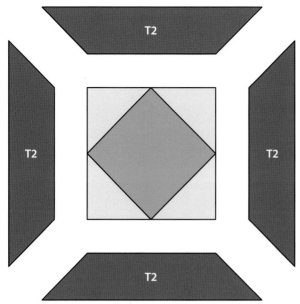

2. Pin and sew four T2 pieces to each T5 edge and then stitch them together at the corners.

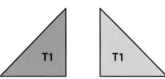

3. Pin and sew two T1 pieces along one short side. Repeat to make four.

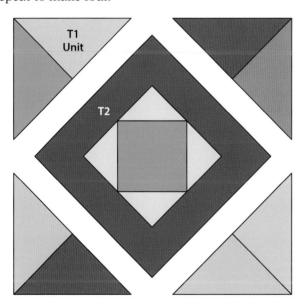

4. Pin and sew a joined T1 unit to each T2 edge. Repeat to make 28.

Block Two Assembly Diagram

CONSTRUCTION

1. Following the Quilt Layout Diagram, arrange the blocks in rows on point. Start with a Block One in the top left corner, then alternate Block Two and Block One across the quilt.

2. Add a background block in between each pieced block, then add the background T6 setting triangles to the end of each diagonal row and the four background T7 corner triangles to each corner.

3. Sew the blocks together, then sew the diagonal rows together to complete the quilt top.

4. Baste and quilt as desired. (I used DMC Size 8 Cotton Perle Thread in Col 353 to hand quilt.) Bind using the instructions in the Finishing Your Quilt section on page 107.

Quilt Layout Diagram

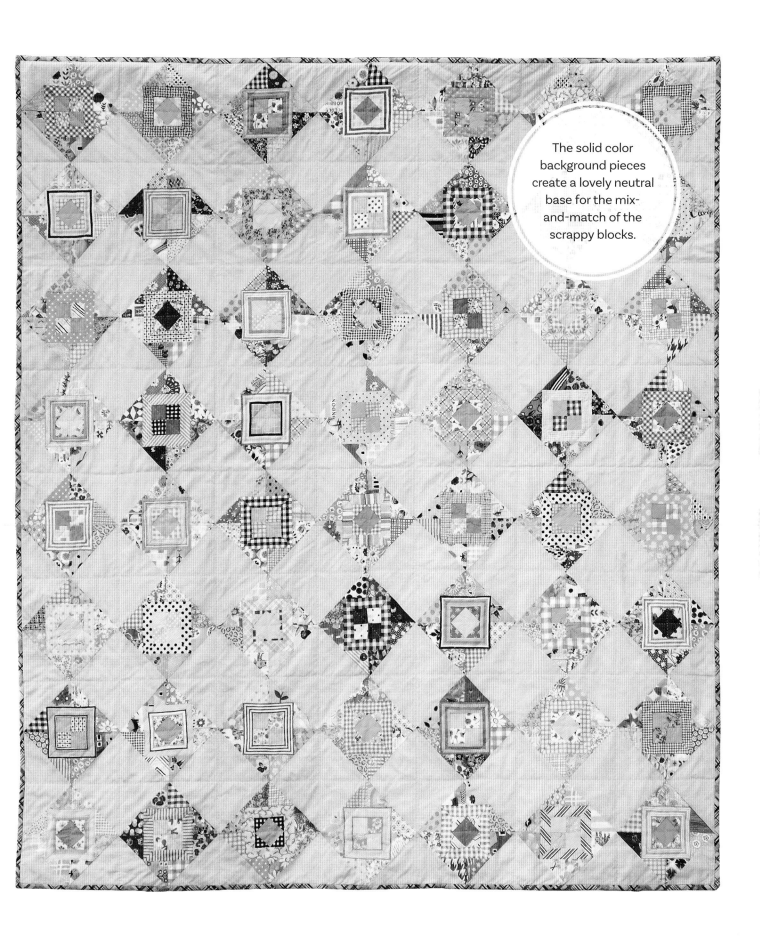

The solid color background pieces create a lovely neutral base for the mix-and-match of the scrappy blocks.

Happy May Day

May Day celebrates the return of spring in the Northern Hemisphere, and it was once customary to give out May baskets to loved ones filled with flowers and homemade treats. The first of May is also my birthday, so I had to make a fun basket quilt, filled with some gorgeous bright and bold patterns and my favorite shade of green! The prairie points replicate the triangles in the baskets and give the quilt a bold but fun finish.

FINISHED QUILT SIZE: 70" (177.8cm) square
FINISHED BLOCK SIZE: 10" (25.4cm) square (10½" [26.7cm] square including seam allowance)

REQUIREMENTS

- Fat sixteenth of bright patterned fabric for each basket—24 total
- Fat sixteenth of coordinating solid color fabric for each basket—24 total
- 1⅛ yds. (1m) background fabric for basket blocks
- 2¼ yds. (2.1m) solid color fabric for alternate block
- 1⅓ yds. (1.2m) gingham fabric for handles and prairie points
- 4½ yds. (4.1m) facing and backing fabric
- 78" (2m) square batting
- ½" (1.3cm) bias tape maker
- Template on page 112
- Rotary cutter
- Cutting mat
- Coordinating cotton thread
- Ruler
- Template plastic
- Fine permanent marker

PREPARATION

Using the ½" (1.3cm) bias tape maker, make up 24 handles using the gingham fabric strips.

Make the templates by tracing them onto the template plastic using a fine permanent marker. Cut them out on the line and label them with their numbers.

CUTTING INSTRUCTIONS

For Basket Block (24 blocks total), and including gingham fabric handles below

- From the bright patterned fabrics, cut:
  - One 4½" (11.4cm) square
  - Two 2½" (6.4cm) squares
- From the coordinating solid color fabrics, cut:
  - Three 2⅞" (7.3cm) squares, cross-cut diagonally into two triangles (6 triangles total)
- From the background fabric for all basket blocks, cut:
  - Twelve 8⅞" (22.5cm) squares, cross-cut diagonally into two triangles (24 triangles total)
  - Twelve 4⅞" (12.2cm) squares, cross-cut diagonally into two triangles (24 triangles total)
  - Forty-eight 6½" x 2½" (16.5 x 6.4cm) rectangles

- From the solid color fabric for alternate blocks, cut:
  - Twenty-five 10½" (26.7cm) squares
- From the gingham fabric, cut:
  - Twenty-four 1" x 11" (2.5 x 27.9cm) strips on the bias for handles
  - Seventy-two 4½" (11.4cm) squares for prairie points
- From the facing and backing fabric, cut:
  - Two 70½" x 1¾" (179.1 x 4.4cm) strips down the length of the fabric
  - Two 69½" x 1¾" (176.5 x 4.4cm) strips down the length of the fabric
  - The remainder is for the backing

MAKE THE BASKET BLOCK

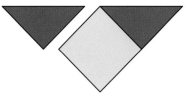

1. Stitch a solid color triangle on either side of a 2½" (6.4cm) patterned square. Repeat to make two units.

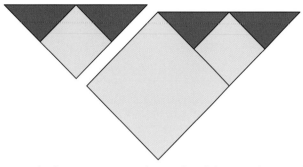

2. Stitch these units to either side of the 4½" (11.4cm) patterned square to make the basket.

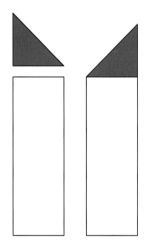

3. Stitch one of the remaining solid color triangles to a background rectangle. Repeat with the other triangle and rectangle, with the triangle facing the opposite direction to form the basket base.

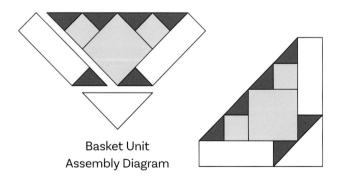

Basket Unit
Assembly Diagram

4. Stitch the combined rectangle and triangle units along either side of the basket, then add the small background triangle to the bottom.

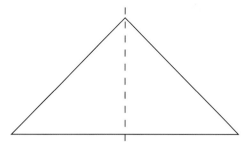

5. Press the large background triangle in half and crease to find the center point.

TIP
With a quilt clip, bundle the solid pieces and print pieces for each basket so everything is organized prior to stitching.

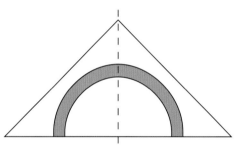

6. Line the HMD1 template along the center point and straight edge. Draw a line around the template onto the background piece to mark the outside edge of the handle. Pin a ½" (1.3cm) bias strip along the line and appliqué it onto the background to make the basket handle.

7. Stitch the handle unit to the basket unit to complete the basket block.

CONSTRUCTION

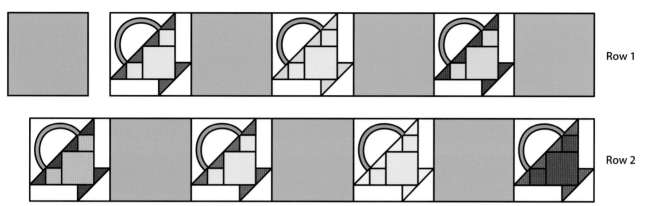

Row 1

Row 2

1. Lay out the rows, alternating the plain blocks with the basket blocks. Row 1 has four plain blocks and three basket blocks and row 2 has four basket blocks and three plain blocks. Stitch the blocks together and repeat to make seven rows.

2. Stitch the rows together.

3. Baste and quilt as desired. Trim the batting and backing to the edge of the quilt top.

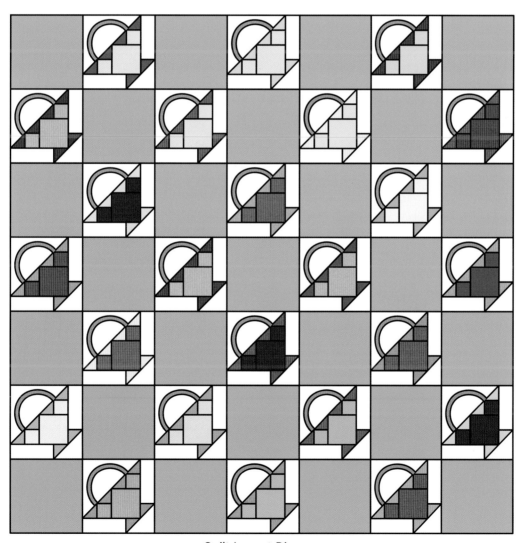

Quilt Layout Diagram

ADD THE PRAIRIE POINTS

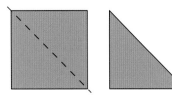

1. Fold a 4" (10.2cm) square in half and then in half again and press. Repeat to make 72 folded triangles (prairie points).

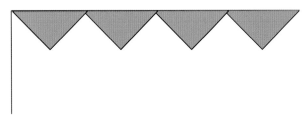

2. Starting at one corner, pin 18 prairie points side by side along one quilt edge, spreading them evenly and tucking the first one in between the layers of the second one.

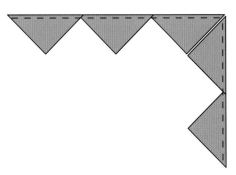

3. Start the next edge of the quilt by aligning the first prairie point with the last prairie point of the previous edge. Continue down the next edge of the quilt. Continue with the other two sides of the quilt. Stitch the prairie points down with a longer basting stitch to hold them in place.

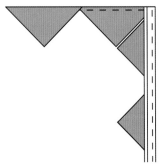

4. Press facing strips under ½" (1.2 cm) along the length. With the right side facing the quilt front, stitch the unpressed side to the quilt and prairie points. Repeat along the opposite edge of the quilt.

5. Press both facing strips outward and then to the back of the quilt so the facing will lay flat to the back of the quilt when it is finished.

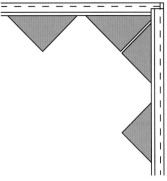

6. Pin another facing strip ½" (1.2 cm) away from the corner and with the right side facing the quilt front, then stitch from edge to edge. Repeat with the remaining quilt edge.

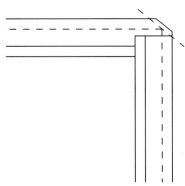

7. Stitch each corner of the quilt diagonally through the intersecting seams in the seam allowance. Trim the corners to the stitching line. This strengthens the corner but removes the bulk of the seam allowance.

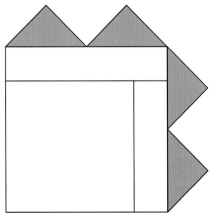

8. Turn the facings to the back of the quilt and slip stitch them in place. Give the edges a light press to make sure the prairie points are sitting nice and flat.

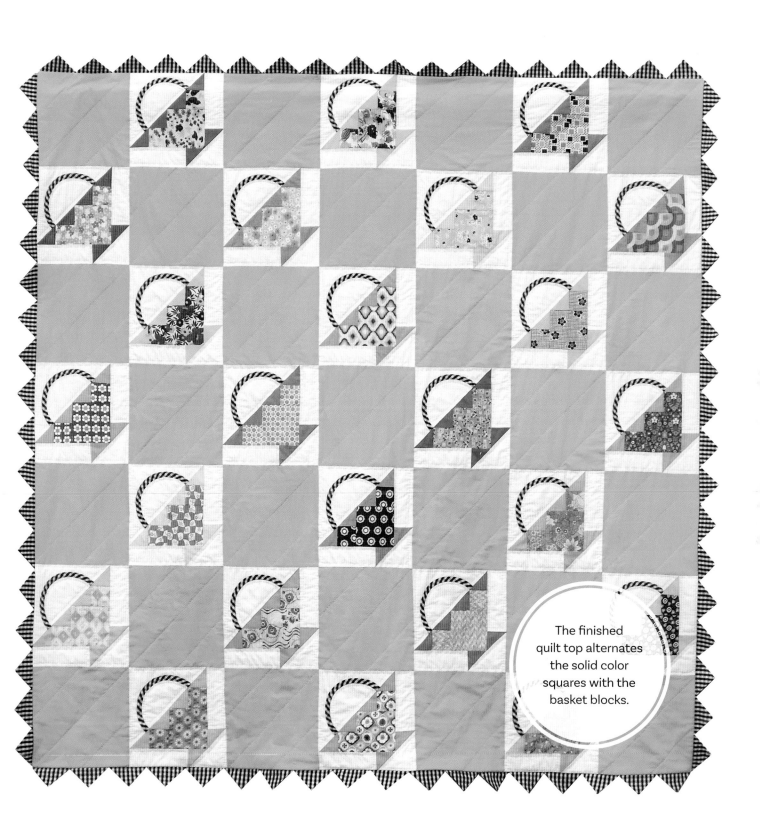

The finished quilt top alternates the solid color squares with the basket blocks.

Hyacinth

Although appearing in earlier quilts, the Dresden Plate Block hit peak popularity in the 1920s and 30s. Thought to have been named after the beautifully painted porcelain from Dresden, Germany, they were made from many bright, colorful flour sack prints with both pointed or round edges or even a combination of both. For this gorgeous quilt, I have used traditional pastels and a wide sashing for a 1930s look and a split floral and solid blade for the Dresden Plate to give it movement. This quilt includes rotary cutting, using a template for the Dresden Plate. It can be pieced by hand or machine.

FINISHED QUILT SIZE: 64" (162.5cm) square

REQUIREMENTS

- 2 yds. (1.8m) floral fabric for the Dresden Plate Blocks and binding
- 2¾ yds. (2.5m) solid blue fabric for Dresden Plate Blocks and sashing
- 2⅜ yds. (2.2m) solid pale pink fabric for background
- ⅓ yd. (30.5cm) solid bright pink fabric for posts
- 4 yds. (3.7m) backing fabric
- 72" (1.9m) square batting
- Template on page 113
- Template plastic
- Fine permanent marker
- 2B pencil or ceramic lead fabric pencil
- Coordinating cotton thread
- Ruler
- Rotary cutter
- Cutting mat

PREPARATION

Make the templates by tracing them onto the template plastic using a fine permanent marker. Cut them out on the line and label them with their numbers.

CUTTING INSTRUCTIONS

- From the floral fabric, cut:
  - Twenty-one 2¼" (5.7cm) x WOF strips for Dresden Plate Blocks
  - Six 2½" (6.4cm) x WOF strips for binding
- From the solid blue fabric, cut:
  - Twenty-one 2¼" (5.7cm) x WOF strips for Dresden Plate Blocks
  - Twenty-four 16½" x 4½" (42 x 11.4cm) rectangles for sashing
- From the solid pale pink fabric, cut:
  - Nine 16½" (42cm) squares for backgrounds
- From the solid bright pink fabric, cut:
  - Sixteen 4½" (11.4cm) squares for posts

CONSTRUCTION

1. Stitch together a floral fabric strip and a solid blue fabric strip along the long edges. Repeat with the remaining floral and solid blue fabric strips.

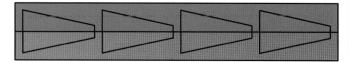

2. Cut 144 copies of template H1, making sure they are all oriented the same way.

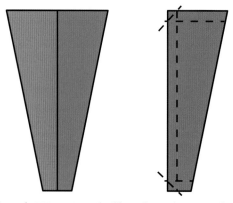

3. Fold each H1 unit in half, right sides together, then stitch across the top and bottom of each. Trim the corners.

4. Turn the H1 units right side out to form points on each end.

5. With right sides together, join sixteen H1 units together to form a circle. This completes your Dresden Plate.

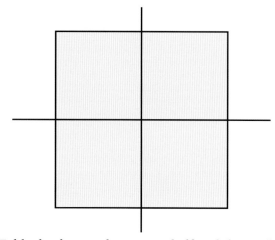

6. Fold a background square in half and then in half again to make a crease to mark the center points of the sides.

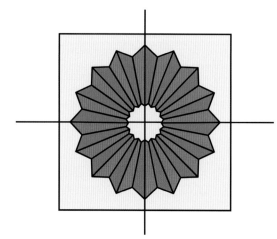

7. Line up the outer and inner points of one of the completed Dresden Plates at each of the crease lines and pin or glue it to the background square. Using your preferred method, appliqué the Dresden Plate to the background square around the outside and inside of the Dresden Plate. Repeat to create the remaining eight blocks.

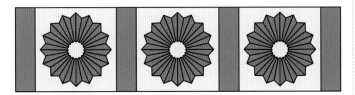

8. Stitch together four vertical sashing strips and three Dresden Plate Blocks as shown. Repeat to make three rows.

9. Stitch together four posts and three horizontal sashing strips as shown. Repeat to make four rows.

10. Alternating sashing and post rows and sashing and Dresden Plate Block rows, stitch together the rows, starting and finishing with a sashing and post row.

11. Baste and quilt as desired. (I used DMC Size 8 Cotton Perle Thread to hand quilt.) Bind using the instructions in the Finishing Your Quilt section on page 107.

Quilt Layout Diagram

Laundrette

This block is inspired by an old Nancy Cabot block she called "Oriental Star." I loved the pieced octagon center, so I upsized it and put it into rows—which reminded me of a laundromat full of washing machines. I love the super scrappy wedges with the low-volume background, but you could also use a single fabric in each octagon and a plain background to create a completely different look.

FINISHED QUILT SIZE: 60½" x 72½" (153.8 x 184cm)
FINISHED BLOCK SIZE: 12" (30.5cm) square (12½" [31.8cm] square with seam allowance)

REQUIREMENTS

- 4¼ yds. (3.9m) assorted patterned fabrics for octagon segments, including stripes, spots, checks, and florals (fat eighths and fat quarters are suitable)
- 1¾ yds. (1.6m) low-volume background fabrics
- 68" x 80" (1.7 x 2m) rectangle batting
- 3⅞ yds. (3.5m) backing fabric
- ½ yd. (45.7cm) binding fabric
- Templates on page 114
- Template plastic
- Fine permanent marker
- 2B pencil or ceramic lead fabric pencil
- Coordinating cotton thread
- Ruler
- Rotary cutter
- Cutting mat

PREPARATION

Make the templates by tracing them onto the template plastic using a fine permanent marker. Cut them out on the line and label them with their numbers.

CUTTING INSTRUCTIONS

For each block (30 blocks total)

- From the patterned fabrics, cut:
  - Eight L2 pieces (240 total)
- From the low-volume background fabrics, cut:
  - One L1 piece (30 total)
  - Four L3 pieces (120 total)

- From the binding fabric, cut:
  - Seven 2½" (6.4cm) x WOF strips

CONSTRUCTION

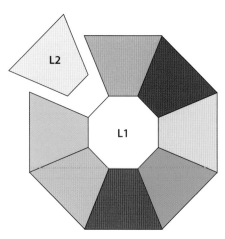

1. Stitch eight L2 wedges around an L1 octagon.

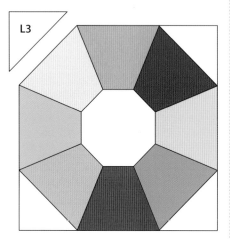

2. Stitch four L3 triangles to every other L2 wedge to add corners and create the block. Repeat to make 30 blocks.

3. Lay out the blocks in six rows of five blocks. Sew the blocks together to create the rows, then sew the rows together to complete the quilt top.

4. Baste and quilt as desired. (I used DMC Size 8 Cotton Perle Thread in Col 959 to hand quilt.) Bind using the instructions in the Finishing Your Quilt section on page 107.

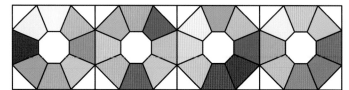

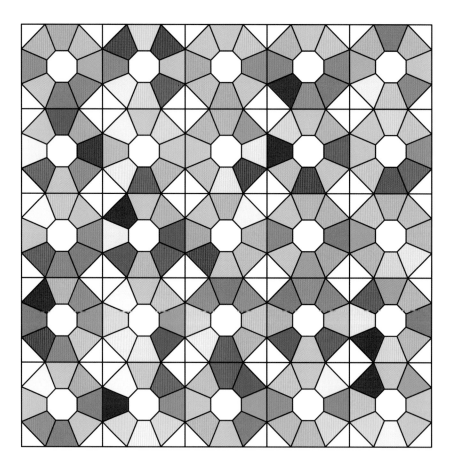

Quilt Layout Diagram

This finished quilt is a whirlwind of movement, color, and texture—like the vintage quilts that inspired it.

Marigold

Yo-yos, or Suffolk puffs, have been around for centuries and likely originated in Suffolk in England. They were stitched together on four sides to make quilts and sometimes were filled with wool to add warmth. Popular during the 1920s to 1940s, they were often pieced into colorful patterns or used as decorative elements on finished quilts or other stitching projects. This pretty cot quilt is template-cut and hand-pieced. The flower blocks are finished with a yo-yo center to add fun texture to a lovely scrappy quilt.

FINISHED QUILT SIZE: 40" (101.6cm) square
FINISHED BLOCK SIZE: 8" (20.3cm) square (8½" [21.6 cm] square including seam allowance)

REQUIREMENTS

- ⅝ yd. (57.2cm) assorted floral fabrics
- 1¼ yds. (114.3cm) assorted bright patterned fabrics
- ⅝ yd. (57.2cm) assorted background fabrics
- ⅝ yd. (57.2cm) border fabric
- 1¼ yds. (114.3cm) backing fabric
- ¾ yd. (68.6cm) binding fabric
- Templates on page 115
- Template plastic
- Fine permanent marker
- 2B pencil or ceramic lead fabric pencil
- Coordinating cotton thread
- Ruler
- Rotary cutter
- Cutting mat

PREPARATION

Make the templates by tracing them onto the template plastic using a fine permanent marker. Cut them out on the line and label them with their numbers.

CUTTING INSTRUCTIONS

- From the assorted floral fabrics, cut:
  - Sixty-four M1 pieces
  - Sixteen M6 pieces
- From the assorted bright patterned fabrics, cut:
  - Sixty-four M2 pieces
  - Sixty-four M3 pieces
  - Sixty-four reversed M3 pieces (see the note on page 14)
- From the assorted background fabrics, cut:
  - Sixty-four M4 pieces
  - Sixty-four reversed M4 pieces (see the note on page 14)
  - Sixty-four M5 pieces
- From the border fabric, cut:
  - Two 4½" x 32½" (11.4 x 82.5cm) rectangles
  - Two 4½" x 40½" (11.4 x 102.9cm) rectangles
- From the binding fabric, cut:
  - Four 2½" (6.4cm) x WOF strips

CONSTRUCTION

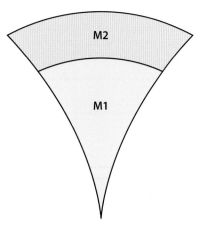

1. Stitch an M2 piece to an M1 piece.

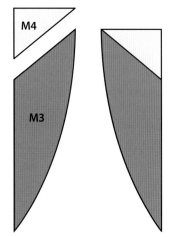

2. Stitch an M4 piece to the top of an M3 piece and a reversed M4 piece to the top of a reversed M3 piece.

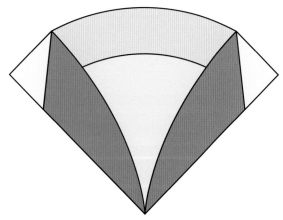

3. Stitch an M3/M4 unit and a reversed M3/M4 unit on either side of the M1/M2 unit.

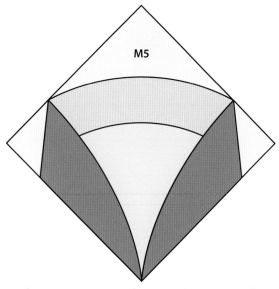

4. Stitch an M5 piece to the top edge to complete a quarter of the block. Repeat to make four quarters.

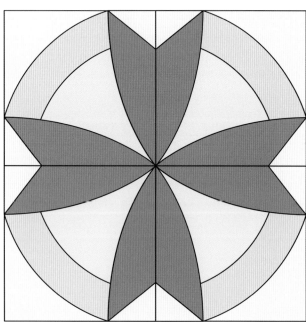

5. Stitch the four quarters together to complete the block. Repeat to make 16 blocks total.

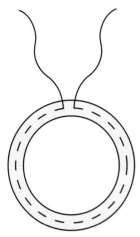

6. Bring your needle up from the back of an M6 circle. Leaving a 3" (7.6cm) tail, baste ¼" (6.4mm) around the edge toward the wrong side of the fabric.

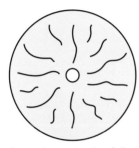

7. Pull the threads to draw in the fabric until it comes together, and then flatten it out, leaving a hole in the center. Distribute the gathers evenly around the center, tie off the threads, and take them through to the back of the yo-yo. Make 16 yo-yos total.

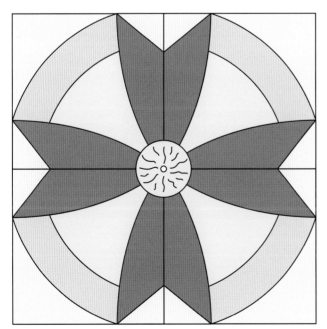

8. Stitch a coordinating floral yo-yo to the center of each block. I stitched through the center and then underneath about ¼" (6.4mm) away from the edge so that the edge is left unattached.

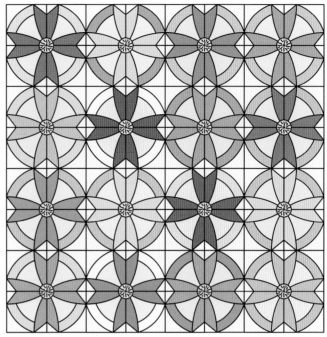

9. Lay out the blocks in four rows of four, balancing the scrappy colors. Stitch the blocks together to form rows, then stitch the rows together to form the quilt top.

10. Stitch a short border to the right and left edges of the quilt top and a long border to the top and bottom edges.

11. Baste and quilt as desired. Bind using the instructions in the Finishing Your Quilt section on page 107.

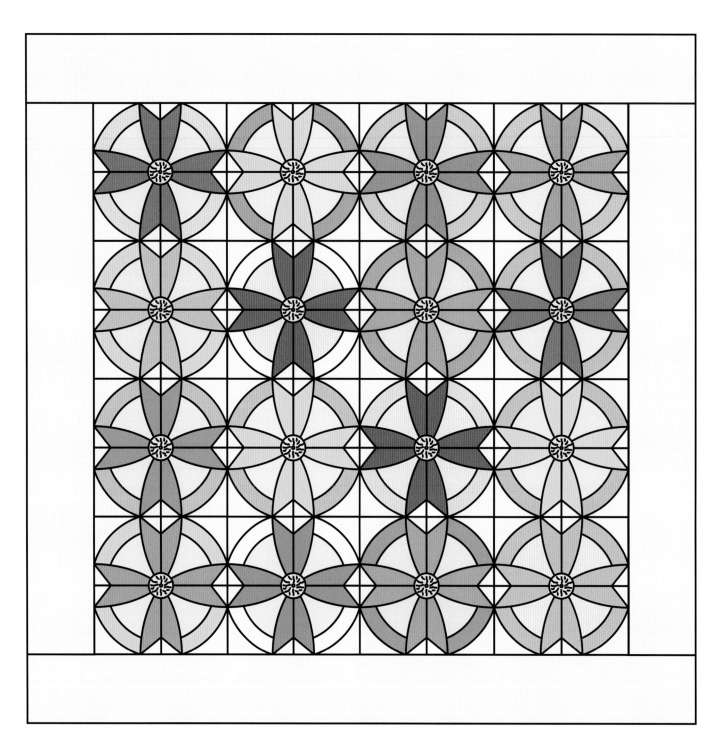

Quilt Layout Diagram

This fresh take on early quilts mixes classic blocks, yo-yos, and a variety of fabric colors and patterns.

Star Lineup

Stars are endlessly popular in quilting either as whole-quilt star designs or single star blocks. Probably the most popular star block is the sawtooth star, named in the late 1800s after its similarity to the teeth on a saw. Playing with a mix of scrappy light and dark fabrics to get a fun striped effect, this quilt would be perfect for the boys in your life. It is rotary-cut and machine-pieced.

FINISHED QUILT SIZE: 72" (182.9cm) square
FINISHED BLOCK SIZE: 8" (20.3cm) square (8½" [21.6 cm] square including seam allowance)

REQUIREMENTS

- 3½ yds. (3.2m) assorted dark fabrics
- 3½ yds. (3.2m) assorted light fabrics
- 4½ yds. (4.1m) backing fabric
- 80" (203.2cm) square batting
- ⅝ yd. (57.2cm) binding fabric
- 2B pencil or ceramic lead fabric pencil
- Coordinating thread
- Sewing machine
- Ruler
- Rotary cutter
- Cutting mat

CUTTING INSTRUCTIONS

For the Half-Square Triangle Blocks (40 blocks total)

- From the assorted light fabrics, cut:
  - Twenty 9½" (24.1cm) squares
- From the assorted dark fabrics, cut:
  - Twenty 9½" (24.1cm) squares

For the Sawtooth Star Blocks (41 blocks total):

- From the assorted light fabrics, cut:
  - Twenty 5½" (14cm) squares
  - Eighty-four 3" (7.6cm) squares
  - Eighty-four 2½" (6.4cm) squares
  - Twenty 4½" (11.4cm) squares
- From the assorted dark fabrics, cut:
  - Twenty-one 5½" (14cm) squares
  - Eighty 3" (7.6cm) squares
  - Eighty 2½" (6.4cm) squares
  - Twenty-one 4½" (11.4cm) squares

- From the binding fabric, cut:
  - Eight 2½" (6.4cm) x WOF strips

MAKE THE HALF-SQUARE TRIANGLE BLOCKS

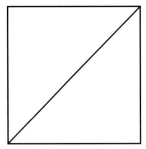

1. Using a pencil, mark all the light 9½" (24.1cm) fabric squares diagonally from corner to corner on the wrong side.

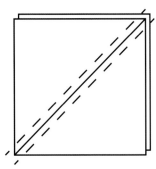

2. Place a light fabric square and a dark fabric square right sides together. Stitch along either side of the marked line, using a ¼" (6.4mm) seam allowance.

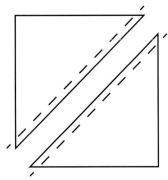 

3. Cut the squares in half along the marked line. Press to set the seam, then open and press the seam toward the dark side. Repeat with the remaining light and dark 9½" (24.1cm) squares to make 40 Half-Square Triangle Blocks total. Trim them to measure 8½" (21.6cm).

MAKE THE SAWTOOTH STAR BLOCKS

1. Start with one 5½" (14cm) dark fabric square and four 3" (7.6cm) light fabric squares. Use a pencil to mark all four of the light squares diagonally from corner to corner on the wrong side.

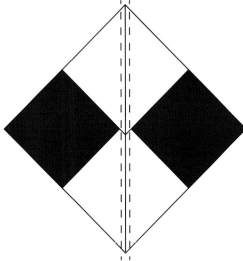

2. With right sides together, pin two light fabric squares in opposite corners of the dark fabric square, slightly overlapping in the center. Stitch along either side of the marked line, using a ¼" (6.4mm) seam allowance.

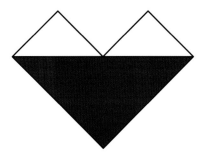

3. Cut the squares in half along the marked line. Press the two units to set the seam, then open and press the seam toward the two smaller triangles.

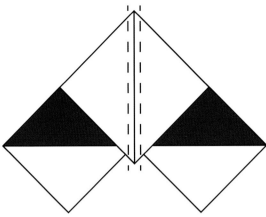

4. Place another light fabric square right sides together on the corner of the large triangle of one of the units. Stitch along either side of the marked line, using a ¼" (6.4mm) seam allowance.

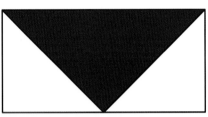

5. Cut the unit in half along the marked line. Press to set the seam, then open and press the seam toward the two smaller triangles. Repeat with the remaining unit. You now have four flying geese units. Trim to measure 2½" x 4½" (6.4 x 11.4cm).

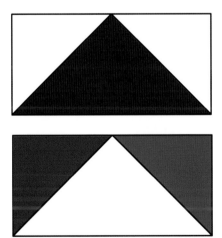

6. Repeat Steps 1 through 5 to make 80 dark background (large triangle) flying geese units and 84 light background (large triangle) flying geese units.

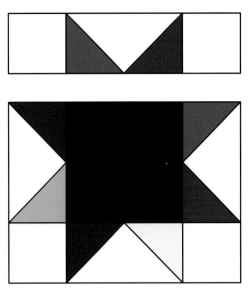

7. Take four 2½" (6.4cm) light squares, one dark 4½" (11.4cm) square, and four light background flying geese units. Piece the block as shown.

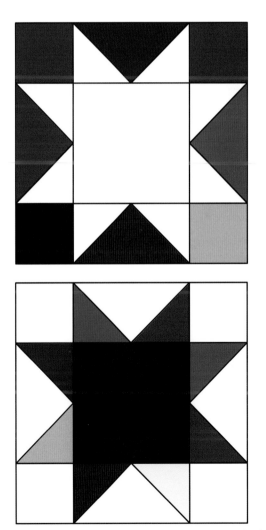

8. Make 21 light background Sawtooth Star Blocks and 20 dark background Sawtooth Star Blocks.

CONSTRUCTION

1. Lay out the completed blocks, alternating the Sawtooth Star Blocks and the Half-Square Triangle Blocks, making sure you follow a diagonal light and dark pattern to achieve stripes diagonally across the quilt.

2. Baste and quilt as desired. (I had this long-arm quilted using a star pattern.) Bind using the instructions in the Finishing Your Quilt section on page 107.

Quilt Layout Diagram

Limit yourself to a few carefully chosen colors, like red, white, and blue, but be creative in mixing shades and patterns within those color families.

The Sunshine Gate

This quilt features my version of a traditional domino block, with the central nine patch replaced with a hexagon. The finished block reminded me of old cast-iron fences and after a little research I found a similar gate manufactured in Australia in the early 20th century by the McKay Sunshine Harvester Works, who also designed the groundbreaking Sunshine Harvester and other agricultural implements. During the 1920s, they were the largest industrial enterprise in the Southern Hemisphere and played a significant role in the mechanization of agriculture around the world. The company had such a huge impact on the area that they renamed it Sunshine. I have used a mixture of greens and sunny yellows with touches of brown and blue to create my gates and brought it all together with a wide floral sashing, another of my favorite features in old quilts.

FINISHED QUILT SIZE: 74" (188cm) square
FINISHED BLOCK SIZE: 10" (25.4cm) square (10½" [26.7cm] square including seam allowance)

REQUIREMENTS

- 4 yds. (3.7m) assorted medium to dark patterned fabrics, including stripes, spots, checks, and florals (fat sixteenths and fat eighths will work)
- 1¾ yds. (1.6m) assorted light patterned fabrics
- ⅜ yd. (34.3cm) floral fabric for short sashing
- 1½ yds. (137.3cm) floral fabric for long sashing and borders
- 4⅝ yds. (4.2m) backing fabric
- ⅝ yd. (57.2cm) binding fabric
- 87" (2.2m) square batting
- Templates on page 116
- Template plastic
- Fine permanent marker
- 2B pencil or ceramic lead fabric pencil
- Size 8 perle cotton thread
- Coordinating cotton thread
- Ruler
- Rotary cutter
- Cutting mat

PREPARATION

Make the templates by tracing them onto the template plastic using a fine permanent marker. Cut them out on the line and label them with their numbers.

CUTTING INSTRUCTIONS

For each block (36 blocks total)

- From the assorted medium to dark patterned fabrics, cut:
  - One TSG1 piece (36 total)
  - Two TSG2 pieces (72 total)
  - Two TSG3 pieces (72 total)
  - Two TSG4 pieces (72 total)
  - Four TSG5 pieces (144 total)
- From the assorted light fabrics, cut:
  - Two TSG4 pieces (72 total)

- From the short sashing fabric, cut:
  - Six 3½" x 20½" (8.9 x 52.1cm) strips
- From the long sashing and border fabric, cut:
  - Four 3½" (8.9cm) x WOF strips, joined to make two 3½" x 66½" (8.9 x 168.9cm) strips
  - Four 4½" (11.4cm) x WOF strips, joined to make two 4½" x 66½" (11.4 x 168.9cm) strips
  - Four 4½" (11.4cm) x WOF strips, joined to make two 4½" x 74½" (11.4 x 189.2cm) strips
- From the binding fabric, cut:
  - Eight 2½" (6.4cm) x WOF strips

CONSTRUCTION

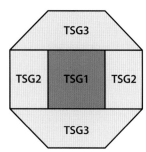

1. Stitch TSG2 pieces to either side of a TSG1 piece, and then stitch TSG3 pieces along their long edges to the top and bottom of the unit.

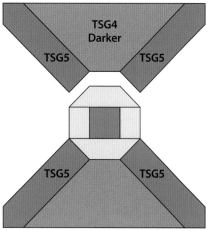

2. Stitch TSG5 pieces to either side of a darker TSG4 piece, then repeat to make two units. Stitch these units to the top and bottom of the TSG1/TSG2/TSG3 unit from Step 1.

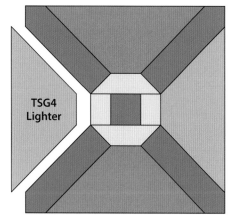

3. Stitch light TSG4 pieces to either side to complete the block. Repeat to make 36 blocks.

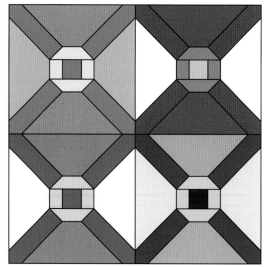

4. Stitch four blocks together. Repeat to make nine four-block units.

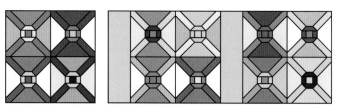

5. Stitch together three four-block units and two vertical sashing strips as shown. Repeat to make three rows.

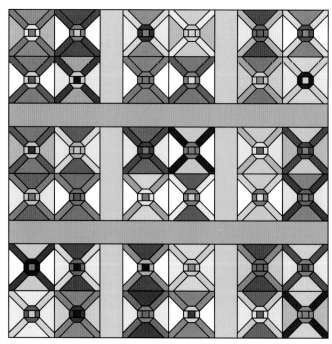

6. Stitch the rows together with a long sashing strip in between each.

Borders and bindings are excellent opportunities for adding more color and texture to round out a quilt design.

7. Stitch the two shorter border strips onto the top and bottom edges, and then stitch the longer border strips to the right and left edges to complete your quilt top.

8. Baste and quilt as desired. (I used DMC Size 8 Cotton Perle Thread in Col 3348 to hand quilt in an all-over Baptist Fan pattern.) Bind using the instructions in the Finishing Your Quilt section on page 107.

Quilt Layout Diagram

Scrappy Projects

Making quilts always leaves us with riches of scraps and extra yardage, so gather up your leftovers and get started on one of these colorful pillows or a vibrant hexagon bag.

Oasis Pillow

This colorful pillow was designed for a dear friend who has a beautiful home filled with an eclectic mix of treasures from her wonderful adventures around the world. It includes some fun Art Deco influences with the palm tree and leopard appliqués and lots of rich colors, patterns, and quilting.

FINISHED PILLOW SIZE: 23" x 16" (58.4 x 40.6cm)

REQUIREMENTS

- Fat quarter gold and pink large-patterned fabric for background
- 12" x 5" (30.5 x 12.7cm) rectangle gold and black dotted fabric for background
- Fat eighth pink patterned fabric for background
- 6" (15.2cm) square orange/pink fabric for background
- 20" x 4" (50.8 x 10.2cm) rectangle black checked fabric for background
- 12" x 3" (30.5 x 7.6cm) rectangle green floral or striped fabric for palm trunk
- Fat sixteenth animal print fabric for leopard
- ⅜ yd. (34.3cm) assorted patterned fabrics for pieced side borders, sun, and palm leaves and coconuts
- ½ yd. (45.7cm) lining fabric
- 30" x 22" (76.2 x 55.9cm) rectangle batting
- ½ yd. (45.7cm) backing fabric
- 18" (45.7cm) zipper
- Templates on pages 117–118
- Template plastic
- Fine permanent marker
- 2B pencil or ceramic lead fabric pencil
- Size 8 variegated perle cotton thread
- 16" x 23" (40.6 x 58.4cm) pillow insert
- Ruler
- Rotary cutter
- Cutting mat

PREPARATION

Make the templates by tracing them onto the template plastic using a fine permanent marker. Cut them out on the line and label them with their numbers.

CUTTING INSTRUCTIONS

Rotary-Cut Pieces

- From the black checked fabric, cut:
  - One 19" x 3" (48.3 x 7.6cm) rectangle
- From the gold and pink large-patterned fabric, cut:
  - One 15½" x 10¼" (39.4 x 26cm) rectangle
- From the gold and black dotted fabric, cut:
  - One 10¼" x 4" (25.4 x 10.2cm) rectangle
- From the pink patterned background fabric, cut:
  - One 4¼" x 3" (10.8 x 7.6cm) rectangle
  - One 13½" x 4¼" (34.3 x 10.8cm) rectangle
- From the orange/pink background, cut:
  - One 4¼" x 3½" (10.8 x 8.9cm) rectangle
- From the assorted patterned fabrics, cut:
  - Two 3½" x 3" (8.9 x 7.6cm) rectangles
  - Two 3½" (8.9cm) squares
  - One 4¼" x 3½" (10.8 x 8.9cm) rectangle
- From the backing fabric, cut:
  - One 16½" x 8" (41.9 x 20.3cm) rectangle
  - One 16½" x 18" (41.9 x 45.7cm) rectangle

Template-Cut Pieces

- From the assorted patterned fabrics, cut:
  - Seven O1 pieces
  - Two O2 pieces
  - One O3 piece
  - One O4 piece
  - One O5 piece
  - One O6 piece
  - One O7 piece
  - One O8 piece
  - Two O9 pieces
- From the animal print fabric, cut:
  - One O10 piece
- From the green floral or striped fabric, cut:
  - One O11 piece

CONSTRUCTION

1. Stitch the O1 triangles together to make a strip and add an O2 triangle to both ends.

2. Stitch the assorted patterned fabric pieces together as shown to create a strip.

3. Stitch the pink pieces to either side of the orange/ pink piece. Stitch the gold and black dotted piece to the right side of the gold large-patterned piece.

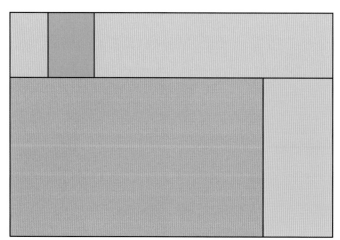

4. Stitch the pink section to the top of the gold section. The background is now ready for the appliqué.

5. Following the diagram and your preferred method, appliqué the palm tree trunk to the background, and then follow with the palm leaves and coconuts. Appliqué on the sun.

6. Stitch the black checked fabric to the bottom edge, the triangle strip to the right edge, and the rectangle strip to the left edge. Appliqué the leopard onto the background along the black checked seam line to complete the pillow front.

7. Baste the pillow front, batting, and lining fabric using your preferred method, and then quilt as preferred. (I used Sue Spargo Eleganza Wonderfil Size 8 perle thread in Variegated Col 25 to hand quilt lines going in different directions and shapes to echo the sun and other elements.) Trim the pillow front to 23½" x 16½" (59.7 x 41.9cm).

FINISH THE PILLOW

1. Use the instructions in the Finishing Your Project section on page 108 to make up your pillow back. Trim the completed back to 23½" x 16½" (59.7 x 41.9cm).

2. Open the zipper halfway to allow turning the pillow cover right side out once the pieces are sewn together. With the right sides together, sew the pillow front to the pillow back, then neaten the edges using a zigzag or overlock stitch.

3. Turn the pillow right side out and stuff it with the pillow insert.

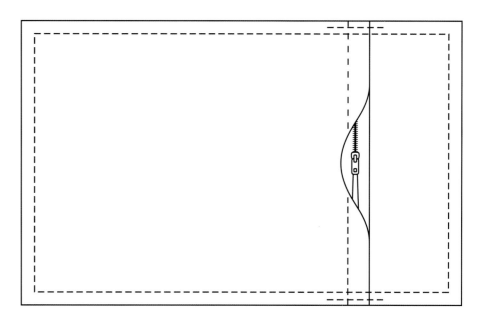

One easy way to add interest to a piece is to break up larger background colors into one or two smaller pieces, like I've done with the pink and gold sections.

Spring Daisies Pillow

Inspired by the bright and bold floral designs of the1970s, this appliqué pillow will add a gorgeous pop of color to any room.

FINISHED PILLOW SIZE: 24½" x 16" (58.4 x 40.6cm)

REQUIREMENTS

- Three fat sixteenths assorted solid color or patterned fabrics for flower petals
- Three 5" (12.7cm) squares assorted patterned fabrics for flower centers
- Three fat sixteenths assorted green solid color or patterned fabrics for stems and leaves
- ½ yd. (45.7cm) low-volume background fabric
- ½ yd. (45.7cm) lining fabric
- 32" x 22" (81.3 x 55.9cm) rectangle batting
- ½ yd (45.7cm) backing fabric
- 18" (45.7cm) zipper
- ¼ yd. (22.9cm) binding fabric
- Size 8 perle cotton thread
- 16" x 25" (40.6 x 63.5cm) pillow insert
- Templates on page 119
- Template plastic
- Fine permanent marker
- 2B pencil or ceramic lead fabric pencil
- Ruler
- Rotary cutter
- Cutting mat

PREPARATION

Make the templates by tracing them onto the template plastic using a fine permanent marker. Cut them out on the line and label them with their numbers.

CUTTING INSTRUCTIONS

Rotary-Cut Pieces

- From the background fabric, cut:
    - One 9" x 16" (22.9 x 40.6cm) rectangle
    - One 6½" x 16" (16.5 x 40.6cm) rectangle
    - One 10" x 16" (25.4 x 40.6cm) rectangle

Template-Cut Pieces

- From each petal fabric, cut:
    - One SD1 piece (3 total)
- From each center fabric, cut:
    - One SD2 piece (3 total)
- From each stem and leaf fabric, cut:
    - Two SD3 pieces (6 total)
    - One 10" x 1" (25.4 x 2.5cm) strip (3 total)
- From the binding fabric, cut:
    - Three 2¼" (5.7cm) x WOF strips

CONSTRUCTION

1. Stitch the background rectangles together along the long edges to create the background.

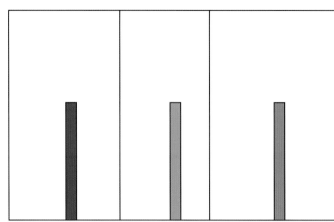

3. Place one stem in the bottom center of the background and then evenly place the two remaining stems on either side. Appliqué them to the background.

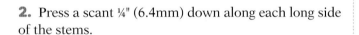

2. Press a scant ¼" (6.4mm) down along each long side of the stems.

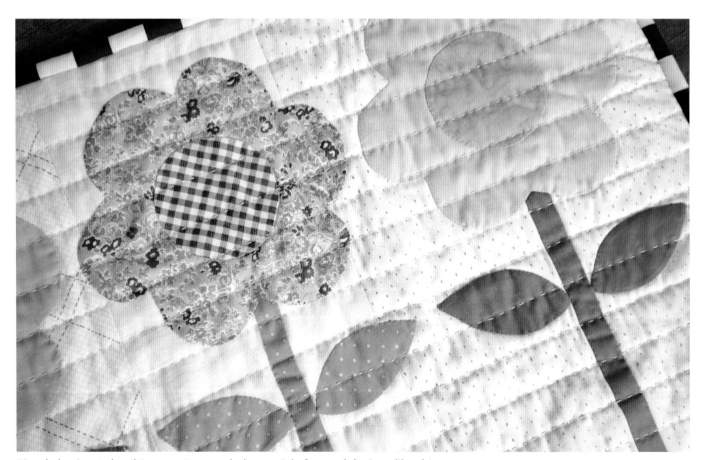

Simple horizontal quilting won't overwhelm straightforward designs like this.

The striped binding perfectly frames the main image on the pillow front without being too heavy.

4. Using needle-turn appliqué or your preferred method, stitch the petals and leaves to the background. Then appliqué the centers onto the petals.

5. Baste the pillow front, batting, and lining fabric using your preferred method, and then quilt as preferred. (I used Size 8 perle thread to hand quilt horizontal lines.) Trim the pillow front to 24½" x 16½" (62.2 x 41.9cm).

FINISH THE PILLOW

1. Use the instructions in the Finishing Your Project section on page 108 to make up your pillow back. Trim the completed back to 24½" x 16½" (62.2 x 41.9cm).

2. Lay the completed pillow back right side down on a flat surface, then lay the pillow front right side up on top of the back, lining up all the edges. Stitch around the pillow close to the edge. This will hold the layers together when you stitch your binding on.

3. Bind using the instructions in the Finishing Your Quilt section on page 107. Stuff with the pillow insert.

Peppermint Christmas Pillow

I love decorating for Christmas and pillows are such an easy way to add a colorful pop of festive cheer to any room. This pillow uses the English paper piecing method, which provides a lovely lacy effect to this bold design.

FINISHED PILLOW SIZE: 20" (50.8cm) square

REQUIREMENTS

- ⅝ yd. (57.2cm) background fabric
- ⅜ yd. (34.3cm) hexagon and diamond fabric
- ½ yd. (45.7cm) backing fabric
- One hundred ½" (1.3cm) hexagon English paper piecing papers
- Six 1" (2.5cm) six-point diamond English paper piecing papers
- 24" (61cm) zipper
- Glue stick (optional)
- Appliqué glue (optional)
- Coordinating cotton thread
- Size 8 perle cotton thread
- Ruler
- Rotary cutter
- Cutting mat
- Hera marker or painter's tape

CUTTING INSTRUCTIONS

- From the background fabric, cut:
  - One 22½" (57.2cm) square
- From the backing fabric, cut:
  - One 15" x 21½" (38.1 x 54.6cm) rectangle
  - One 9½" x 21½" (24.1 x 54.6cm) rectangle

Note: cut these pieces with the 21½" (54.6cm) lengths side by side to make sure the fabric direction is the same for both.

This design gets straight to the point: peppermint colors with a beautiful classic star in the middle!

CONSTRUCTION

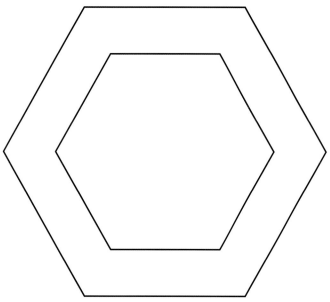

1. From the hexagon fabric, cut your hexagons a generous ¼" (6.4mm) larger than the hexagon paper using the paper as a guide. If you want to glue-baste your hexagons, go to step 2a. If you want to thread-baste your hexagons, go to step 2b.

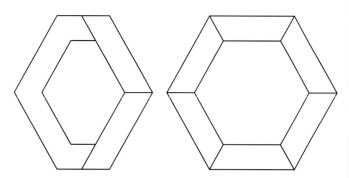

2a. To glue-baste, place the hexagon paper in the middle of the wrong side of the cut fabric hexagon. Dab the fabric with the glue stick along each edge and press onto the paper. Give it a nice sharp edge, but make sure the edges are not too firm so you can stitch them together. Repeat for all hexagon papers.

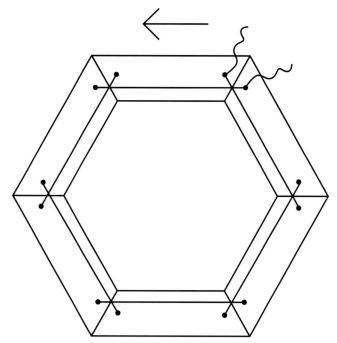

2b. To thread-baste, place the hexagon in the middle of the wrong side of the cut fabric hexagon. Fold one side in toward the back and then fold the next edge down. Start your basting stitch in the fold at the hexagon point, then continue folding each edge in and make basting stitches through each folded corner. Repeat for all hexagon papers.

3. Repeat step 2a or 2b for all six-pointed diamond papers and place them aside until the hexagon star is appliquéd to the background in step 7.

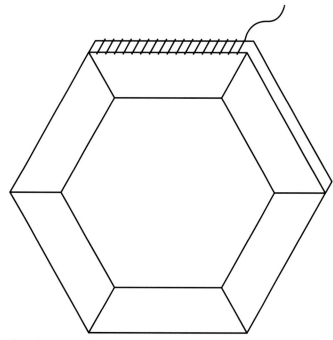

4. Place two hexagons right sides together to join them with a whipstitch. Insert your needle through the corners of both hexagons. Leave a 1" (2.5cm) tail and insert your needle again, this time taking your needle through the loop to create a knot. Take your needle over to the back hexagon and insert your needle back toward you through the edge, bringing it through both hexagons. Repeat, making sure your stitches avoid the paper and aren't too close together. You want around 12–16 stitches per inch.

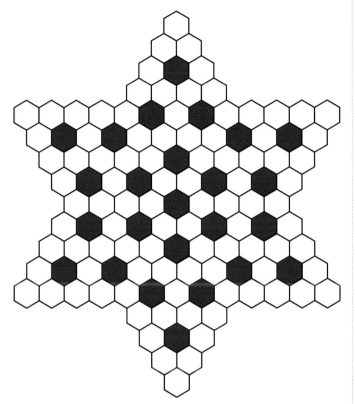

6. Fold your background fabric in half and then in half again to form a crease that marks the center point.

5. Stitch your basted hexagons together following the pattern. Once complete, give both sides of the star a good press, making sure the edges are nice and flat. If you thread-basted, carefully remove the basting stitches and take out the papers. If you glue-basted, carefully peel the glued edges away from the papers and take them out. **Note:** The red in the diagram above indicates where to leave gaps so the background fabric will show through.

7. Lay the completed hexagon star on the background and make sure two of the star points are lined up with the vertical center line on the top and bottom and the inner points on either side line up with the horizontal center line. Pin or glue the star in place and then appliqué it to the background, including all of the hexagon gaps.

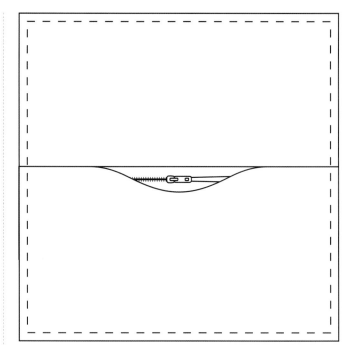

8. Take the basted six-point diamonds, press well, and remove the papers as in Step 5. Appliqué a diamond to each point of the hexagon star as in the pattern. Trim the pillow to 21½" (54.6cm) square. Your pillow top is now complete.

9. Use the instructions in the Finishing Your Project section on page 108 to make up your pillow back. Trim the completed back to 21½" (54.6cm) square.

10. Sew the pillow front and back together using a French seam to enclose the raw edges on the inside seam to stop it from fraying (rather than using an overlocked edge). Lay the pillow back right side down on a flat surface. Lay the pillow front right side up on top of the pillow back. Pin them together carefully and then stitch around the edge using a scant ¼" (6.4mm) seam allowance. Clip the corners to remove the bulk, avoiding cutting into the stitching.

11. Open the zipper and leave it open so you can turn the pillow right side out later. Turn the pillow inside out, so the right sides are now facing. Press the seams flat, pushing out the corners. Stitch around the edges of the pillow again, using a ⅜" (9.5mm) seam allowance. This seam allowance is wider to make sure you cover the first seam. Turn the pillow right side out and push out the corners. Press the seams.

12. Using perle cotton thread, stitch a line 1" (2.5cm) from the edge around the pillow front using a simple running stitch. Use 1" (2.5cm) painter's tape or a Hera marker to mark your line.

Pillow Layout Diagram

Love Bomb Pillow

I originally designed this pillow as a gift for a beautiful friend because it represented what a huge bomb of love I get from her every time we meet. I have remade it to be slightly smaller, using bold hot pink and red and a pretty ruffled trim for a more fun-and-flirty look reminiscent of the colorful 1950s. The pattern includes templates for the background, heart, and block. The background is made up of four blocks using the freezer-paper foundation paper piecing method, and the heart is stitched onto the background using the needle-turn appliqué method. I have also used batting and lining on the pillow front to give it some substance and make it less see-through.

FINISHED PILLOW SIZE: 16" (40.6cm) square
FINISHED BLOCK SIZE: 8" (20.3cm) square (8½" [21.6cm] square including seam allowance)

REQUIREMENTS

- Fat quarter pink solid fabric for background
- Fat quarter cream solid fabric for background
- Fat sixteenth red solid fabric for heart
- ⅝ yd. (57.2cm) coordinating fabric for backing and ruffle trim
- Fat quarter batting
- Fat quarter lining fabric
- 18" (45.7cm) nylon dress zipper
- 18" (45.7cm) square pillow insert
- Templates on pages 120–123
- Template plastic
- ⅜ yd. (34.3cm) freezer paper
- Fine permanent marker
- Coordinating cotton thread
- Ruler
- Rotary cutter
- Cutting mat

PREPARATION

Make the templates by tracing them onto the template plastic using a fine permanent marker. Cut them out carefully on the line and label them with their numbers. The pillow background pieces have an extra cutting line around them as you need extra material for the foundation paper piecing method. If you are hand piecing, just add the normal ¼" (6.4mm) seam allowance.

Trace the block template onto freezer paper. You should be able to use the same paper for all four blocks but make a new one if it stops sticking to the fabric.

CUTTING INSTRUCTIONS

- From the pink solid fabric, cut:
  - Two LB1 pieces
  - Two LB2 pieces
  - Two reversed LB2 pieces (see the note on page 14)
  - Two LB3 pieces
  - Two reversed LB3 pieces (see the note on page 14)
- From the cream solid fabric, cut:
  - Two LB1 pieces
  - Two LB2 pieces
  - Two reversed LB2 pieces (see the note on page 14)
  - Two LB3 pieces
  - Two reversed LB3 pieces (see the note on page 14)
- From the red solid fabric, cut:
  - One LB4 piece

Note: add a generous ⅛" (3.2mm) seam allowance for needle turning.

- From the backing and ruffle trim fabric, cut:
  - Two 3½" (8.9cm) x WOF strips for ruffle trim

Note: cut the ruffle trim first.

  - One 16½" x 8½" (41.9 x 21.6cm) rectangle, for top
  - One 16½" x 11" (41.9 x 27.9cm) rectangle, for bottom

Note: cut the top and bottom pieces with the 16½" (41.9cm) lengths side by side to make sure the fabric direction is the same for both.

- From the batting, cut:
  - One 16½" (41.9cm) square
- From the lining fabric, cut:
  - One 16½" (41.9cm) square

CONSTRUCTION

Note: Make sure you are ironing on the paper side of the freezer paper, not the glue side, as the glue will stick to your iron.

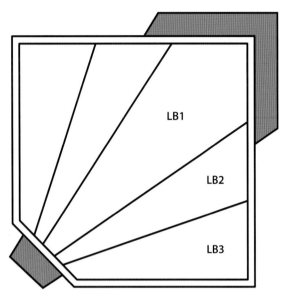

1. With the fabric right side down, press the freezer paper template on an LB1 piece.

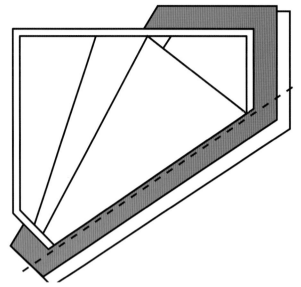

3. Place an LB2 piece of the other color right side facing under the LB1 piece, lining up the edges. Stitch alongside the freezer paper fold.

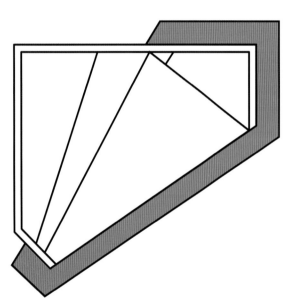

2. Peel back one long edge and fold it along the LB1/LB2 line.

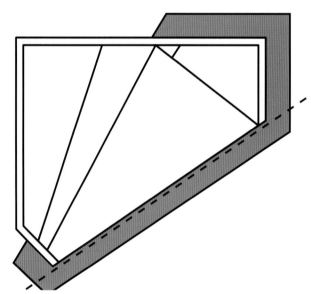

4. Trim the seam to ¼" (6.4cm).

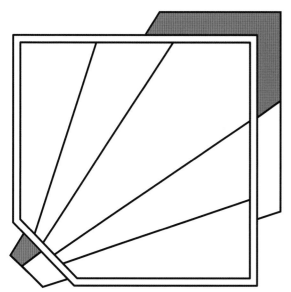

5. Unfold and press the freezer paper back down over the combined pieces.

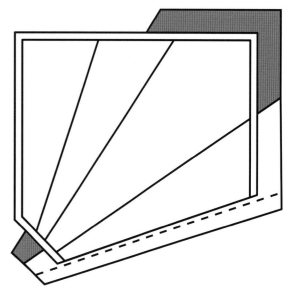

7. Trim the seam to ¼" (6.4cm).

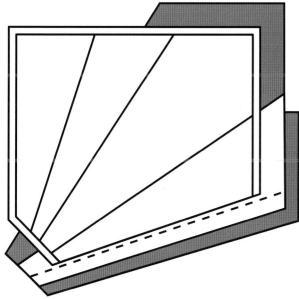

6. Fold back the freezer paper along the LB2/LB3 line. Place an LB3 piece of the first color right side facing under the LB2 piece, lining up the edges. Stitch alongside the freezer paper fold.

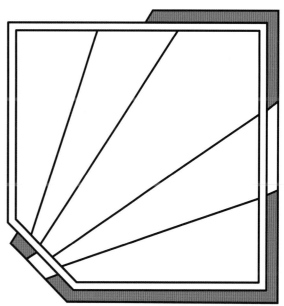

8. Unfold and press the freezer paper back down over the combined pieces.

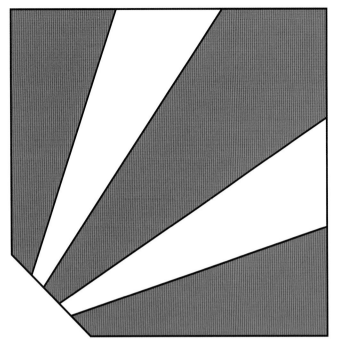

9. Rotate the block and stitch on the reversed LB2 and reversed LB3 pieces using the same method. Trim the block to 8½" (21.6cm) along the outer seam allowance line on the freezer paper.

10. Repeat steps 1 through 9 to make the remaining three blocks. You should have two with pink central LB1 pieces and two with cream central LB1 pieces.

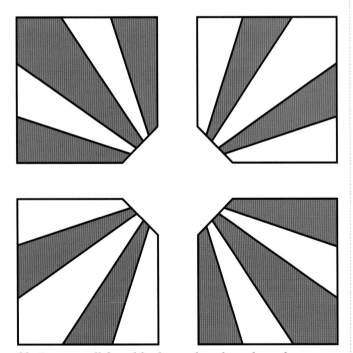

11. Lay out all four blocks so that the colors alternate.

12. Stitch together the top two blocks and repeat with the bottom two blocks. Stitch the joined top and bottom units together to finish the background.

13. Position the LB4 heart piece along the center line, approximately 5½" (14cm) from the bottom of the background. Pin or use appliqué glue to hold it in place and stitch it on using needle-turn appliqué.

14. Cut away any excess background fabric from behind the heart. This will help avoid any show-through of the background.

15. Lay the batting evenly on top of the lining fabric, making sure the edges line up. Then lay the finished pillow front right side up on top of the batting. Baste these three layers together or stay-stitch around the outside edge to keep the layers lined up while you add the ruffle trim.

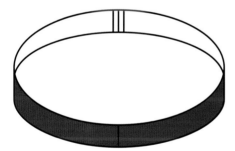

16. To make the ruffle trim, join the two strips at the short end. Making sure the fabric is not twisted, join the other short ends to create a loop. Press the seams open.

17. Press the ruffle strip in half, wrong sides facing, the whole way around the loop.

18. Lay the ruffle strip down with the seams to the left and right. Mark each end with a pin so you have two halves. Change your sewing machine's stitch length to the longest stitch. Leaving a long thread tail (about 5" [12.7cm]), stitch ½" (2.5cm) from the raw edge on one half of the loop, starting at one pin and ending at the other pin. Repeat to add another row of stitching ⅛" (3.2mm) away from the first line of stitching on the raw edge side. Repeat with the other half of the ruffle loop. These are the gathering threads.

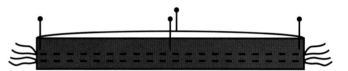

19. Find the halfway point between the two pins and place another pin. Repeat in the other half of the ruffle. This creates quarters, so you can evenly gather the trim for each side of the pillow.

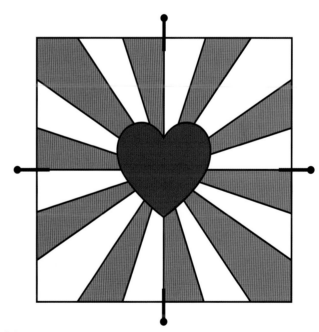

20. Lay your completed pillow top right side up. Find the halfway mark on each side of the pillow front and mark it with a pin.

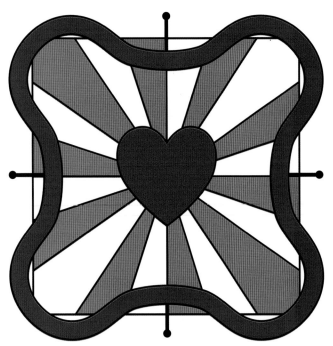

the gathers coming undone. Repeat for the other side of the top and then for the left and right bottom gathering threads until the ruffle is evenly gathered all the way around and pinned to the pillow front.

21. Lay the ruffle along the edge, matching the raw edges and quarter points. Match the pillow center front pin with one of the pins near the gathering threads and pin the two together, removing one of the pins. Repeat with the bottom front center and the other gathering thread pin. Then match and pin the side pins with the quarter-mark pins on the ruffle.

23. Stitch around the pillow using a ¼" (6.4mm) seam allowance. The ½" (1.2cm) gathering thread line will sit outside of this seam but can easily be removed once you have finished sewing the ruffle on. Trim any loose threads.

24. Use the instructions in the Finishing Your Project section on page 108 to make up your pillow back. Trim the completed back to 16½" (41.9cm) square.

25. Open the zipper halfway and leave it open so you can turn the pillow right side out later. With the right sides facing and making sure the ruffles are out of the way, stitch the pillow front and back together using a ¼" (6.4mm) seam allowance. Neaten the seam edges using a zigzag or overlock stitch if you wish. Turn the pillow right side out and stuff with the pillow insert.

22. Take two of the gathering threads on the center top ruffle and start pulling to gather the ruffle on one side. Pull until it gathers to the pin on that side, curving the ruffle as you go around the corner. Make sure the ruffles are even, then pin the ruffle to the pillow front. Wind the threads around the pin to avoid

This pillow pulls together bright colors and striking graphics to convey a different era of vintage design.

Indoor Garden Pillow

We love indoor plants in our house and have them everywhere. They come in all shapes and sizes, which inspired this fun appliqué design. I got carried away with the pot and plant designs, just I like I do with my real plants at home, so this piece turned into a longer lumbar pillow. It would make a great addition to a bed or sofa.

FINISHED PILLOW SIZE: 35½" x 15½" (90.2 x 39.3cm)

REQUIREMENTS

- Five fat sixteenths assorted patterned fabrics for pots
- ⅜ yd. (34.3cm) assorted green fabrics for leaves and stems, including florals, spots, and stripes
- 6" (15.2cm) square orange fabric for pot edge and base
- 5" (12.7cm) square yellow fabric for cactus flowers
- Fat sixteenth brown fabric for stems
- ⅜ yd. (34.3cm) low-volume fabric for background
- 5" (12.7cm) x WOF patterned green fabric for shelf
- ½ yd. (45.7cm) lining fabric
- ½ yd. (45.7cm) backing fabric
- 18" (45.7cm) zipper
- ¼ yd. (22.9cm) binding fabric
- Templates on pages 124–128
- Template plastic
- Fine permanent marker
- 2B pencil or ceramic lead fabric pencil
- ¼" (6.4mm) bias tape maker
- 1 yd. (91.4cm) fabric for pillow insert (calico or homespun work well)
- Two 16" x 25" (40.6 x 63.5cm) pillow inserts or polyester fiber filling to fill pillow insert
- Ruler
- Rotary cutter
- Cutting mat

PREPARATION

Make the templates by tracing them onto the template plastic using a fine permanent marker. Cut them out on the line and label them with their numbers.

CUTTING INSTRUCTIONS

Rotary-Cut Pieces

- From the low-volume background fabric, cut:
  - One 12½" x 35½" (30.5 x 90.2cm) rectangle
- From the shelf fabric, cut:
  - One 3½" x 35½" (8.9 x 90.2cm) rectangle
- From the brown fabric, cut:
  - One ½" x 10" (1.2 x 25.4cm) bias strip
- From one green fabric, cut:
  - One ½" x 10" (1.2 x 25.4cm) bias strip
- From the lining fabric, cut:
  - One 15½" x 35½" (39.4 x 90.2cm) rectangle
- From the backing fabric, cut:
  - One 15½" x 25" (39.4 x 63.5cm) rectangle
  - One 15½" x 13" (39.4 x 33cm) rectangle

The cut fabric "leaves" are layered over each other to create a sense of depth in the image.

- From the binding fabric, cut:
  - Three 2¼"
    (56.5cm) x WOF strips
- From the pillow insert fabric, cut:
  - Two 15½" x 35½"
    (39.4 x 90.2cm) rectangles

Template-Cut Pieces

- From each of the assorted patterned fabrics, cut:
  - One IG1 piece
  - One IG5 piece
  - One IG11 piece
  - One IG17 piece
  - One IG18 piece
  - One IG23 piece
- From the remaining green fabrics, cut:
  - One IG2 piece
  - One IG3 piece
  - One IG4 piece
  - Five IG6 pieces
  - Five IG7 pieces
  - Three IG8 pieces
  - Four IG9 pieces
  - Three IG10 pieces
  - One IG12 piece
  - One IG13 piece
  - One IG14 piece
  - One IG15 piece
  - One IG19 piece
  - One IG20 piece
  - One IG21 piece
  - One IG22 piece
  - One IG26 piece
  - One IG27 piece
  - One IG28 piece
  - One IG29 piece
  - One IG30 piece
- From the orange fabric, cut:
  - One IG24 piece
  - One IG25 piece
- From the yellow fabric, cut:
  - Three IG16 pieces

CONSTRUCTION

1. Stitch your background rectangles together along the long sides to create the background.

2. Make your stems using the ¼" (6.4mm) bias tape maker. Make three from the green fabric strip and four from the brown fabric strip.

3. Using needle-turn appliqué and following the diagram, stitch each potted plant onto the background. The templates for plants 3 and 5 indicate with a dashed line where the shapes will be covered by another shape. To line things up nicely, start with stitching the pots and pot bases along the shelf seam, leaving the top edge of the pots open to add the plants. Then stitch the stems on for plants 1 and 4, followed by the leaves and flowers for all five pots. Finish the pot edges for pots 1, 3, and 4, and then add the top edge to pot 5.

The background and shelf fabric choices should help to emphasize the main focus of the pillow.

FINISH THE PILLOW

1. Use the instructions in the Finishing Your Project section on page 108 to make up your pillow back. Trim the completed back to 35½" x 15½" (90.2 x 38.1cm).

2. Lay the completed pillow back right side down on a flat surface. Lay the lining on top and then lay the pillow front right side up on top of the lining, making sure all the edges line up. Stitch around the pillow close to the edge. This will hold the layers together when you stitch your binding on.

3. Bind the pillow using the instructions in the Finishing Your Project section on page 107.

4. With right sides together, sew the back and front pillow insert pieces together, leaving an opening at one short end to turn the pillow insert right side out.

5. Stuff the pillow insert with feathers pulled out of the smaller pillow inserts (do this outside) or with polyester fiber filling. Sew the opening closed. Place into the finished pillow cover.

Barley Sugar Pillow

This pillow features the versatile Drunkard's Path Block, which is widely believed to have been popular in 1920s to 1930s quilting as a way for women in the United States to promote the abolition of alcohol during the temperance movement. Known by many other names, including Solomon's Puzzle and Wanderer in the Wilderness, these blocks can create some wonderful patterns just by being turned in different directions. I have gone for a fun, scrappy "ribbon" effect in this pillow that would also look very effective in just two colors. The pillow is template-cut, can be hand- or machine-pieced, and features some simple hand quilting.

FINISHED PILLOW SIZE: 18" (45.7cm) square
FINISHED BLOCK SIZE: 3" (7.6cm) square (3½" [8.9cm] square including seam allowance)

REQUIREMENTS

- 10" (25.4cm) assorted bright patterned fabrics, including florals and geometrics
- ⅜ yd. (34.3cm) background fabric
- 20" (50.8cm) square lining fabric
- 20" (50.8cm) square batting
- ⅜ yd. (34.3cm) pillow backing fabric
- ¼ yd. (22.9cm) binding fabric
- 20" (50.8cm) nylon zipper
- Size 8 perle cotton thread
- 18" (45.7cm) pillow insert
- Templates on page 129
- Template plastic
- 2B pencil or ceramic lead fabric pencil
- Fine permanent marker
- Ruler
- Rotary cutter
- Cutting mat

PREPARATION

Make the templates by tracing them onto the template plastic using a fine permanent marker. Cut them out on the line and label them with their numbers.

CUTTING INSTRUCTIONS

- From the mix of bright fabrics, cut:
  - Thirty-six BS1 pieces
- From the background fabric, cut:
  - Thirty-six BS2 pieces
- From the backing fabric, cut:
  - One 18½" x 9½" (45.7 x 24.1cm) rectangle
  - One 18½" x 11½" (45.7 x 28cm) rectangle
- From the binding fabric, cut:
  - Three 2¼" (5.7cm) x WOF strips

MAKE THE BLOCKS

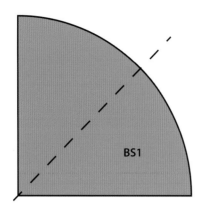

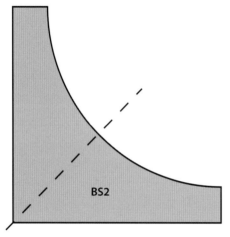

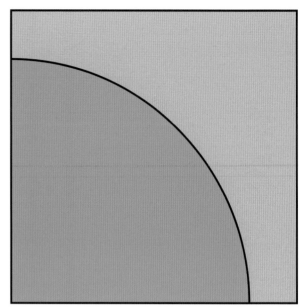

2. With right sides together and the BS2 piece at the front, pin the BS2 piece to the BS1 piece in the marked center points of the curved edge. Pin each end, pin between each end pin and the center pin, then stitch the two pieces together along the curve, easing it to fit. Repeat to make 36 blocks.

1. Fold a BS1 piece in half, bringing the straight edges together. Make a crease to mark the center point of the curve. Repeat with a BS2 piece.

The Drunkard's Path blocks create a lot of motion in a quilt and you can rearrange them to create completely different looks.

FINISH THE PILLOW

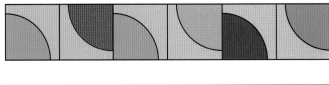

1. Lay six of your completed blocks in a row, alternating the colored BS1 pieces down and then up. Lay another six blocks out, alternating the colored BS1 pieces up and then down. Repeat to complete six rows—three of each arrangement. Stitch the blocks together.

2. Lay out the six rows in alternating order to form the pattern. Stitch the rows together.

3. Baste the pillow front, batting, and lining together, then quilt as desired. (I used Size 8 Cotton Perle Thread to hand quilt lines ¼" [6.4mm] outside the colored shapes to echo them.)

4. Use the instructions in the Finishing Your Project section on page 108 to make up your pillow back. Trim the completed back to 18½" (45.7cm) square.

5. Trim the lining and the batting of your pillow top to the same size as the front. Lay the completed pillow back right side down on a flat surface and then lay the pillow front right side up on top of the back, lining up the edges. Stitch around the pillow using a ⅛" (3.2mm) seam allowance to hold the layers together while you stitch your binding on.

6. Use the binding instructions in the Finishing Your Project section on page 107.

Pillow Layout Diagram

Veronica Bag

You can never have too many project bags! Combining hexagons, gingham, a cute ruffle, and cane handles, the Veronica Bag captures the modern-retro scrappy style.

FINISHED BAG SIZE: 15" x 18" (38.1 x 45.7cm)

REQUIREMENTS

- 1 yd. (91.4cm) assorted bright fabrics, including florals, checks, and geometrics
- 1 yd. (91.4cm) gingham fabric for the lining, handle casings, binding, and frill
- ⅝ yd. (57.2cm) medium iron-on fusible interfacing
- Circular, D-shape, or rectangular bag handles in cane, bamboo, or plastic
- Templates on page 130
- Template plastic
- Fine permanent marker
- 2B pencil or ceramic lead fabric pencil
- Coordinating cotton thread
- Ruler
- Rotary cutter
- Cutting mat

PREPARATION

Make the templates by tracing them onto the template plastic using a fine permanent marker. Cut them out on the line and label them with their numbers.

CUTTING INSTRUCTIONS

Rotary-Cut Pieces

- From the gingham fabric, cut:
  - Two 15½" x 18½" (39.3 x 47cm) rectangles for lining
  - Two 4" x 20½" (10.2 x 52.1cm) rectangles for frills
  - Two 6½" x 13½" (16.5 x 34.3cm) rectangles for handle casings
  - Two 10" x 1⅜" (25.4 x 3.5cm) bias strips

Template-Cut Pieces

- From the assorted bright fabrics, cut:
  - Seventy VB1 pieces
  - Five VB2 pieces

CONSTRUCTION

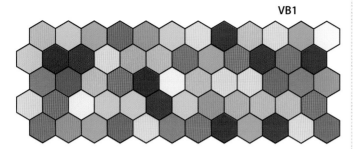

VB1

1. Stitch five rows of twelve hexagon VB1 pieces. Join the rows together.

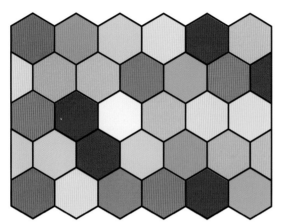

2. Stitch the ends of the hexagon rows together into a tube, creating the sides of the bag.

VB2

3. Stitch two rows of five hexagon VB1 pieces. Stitch one row to the top front and one row to the top back. Stitch the five diamonds onto the bottom front and bottom back hexagons to form the base of the bag. Sew the front and back hexagons together on both bottom corners.

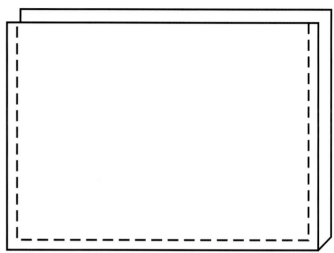

4. Iron the fusible interfacing onto the lining pieces and then stitch them together down the sides and across the bottom.

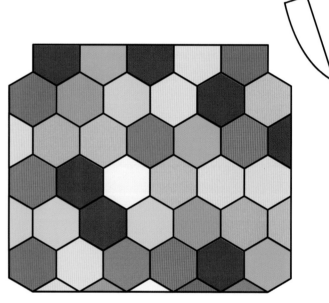

5. With the wrong sides facing, insert the lining into the outer bag. Trim the top of the hexagons into a straight line by removing the triangle section. Use the VB3 template to draw curves on the front top right and left corners of the bag and lining, then cut. Repeat on the other side of the bag.

6. Press ¼" (6.4mm) in toward the wrong side on each long edge of the bias strips.

This bag is a great project for using up small pieces of fabrics you love that might not be large enough for use in a full quilt project.

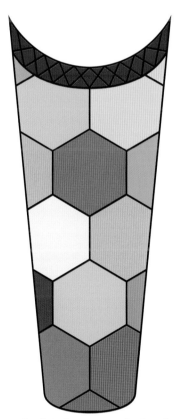

8. With right sides together, press the frill strip in half lengthwise and stitch across the short ends. Turn the piece right side out and press it. Repeat with the other frill strip.

9. Set your machine to the longest stitch length and sew two lines of gathering stitches along the raw edges.

7. Pin and sew the binding onto the bag's side curves.

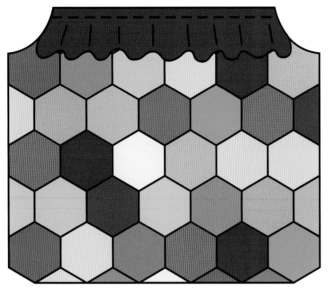

10. Gather the frill until it measures 13" (33cm) and stitch it to the outside front of the bag. Repeat with the other side.

11. With right sides together, fold the handle casing strip in half lengthwise and stitch across the short ends. Turn the piece right side out and press it.

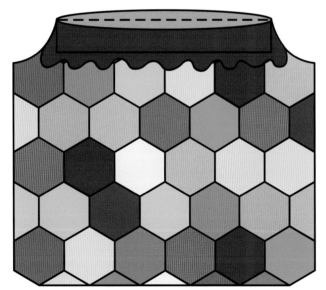

12. Stitch one side of the handle casing to the outside of the bag, leaving the other edge of the casing free. Repeat on the other side with the second casing.

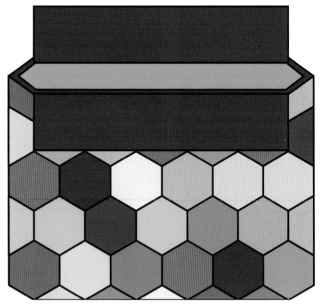

13. Press under the seam allowance on the free casing edge and stitch it to the lining of the bag using a slip stitch. Repeat on the other side with the remaining casing.

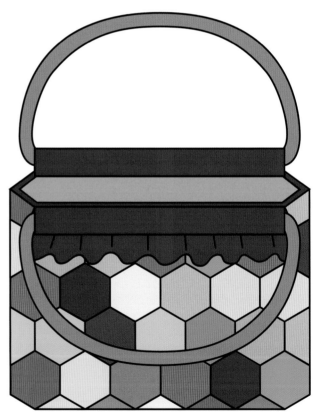

14. Fold the handle casing over the handle, pin it in place, and then stitch it to the lining of the bag using a slip stitch. Repeat with the other handle to complete the bag.

The fabric colors and patterns and handles you use for your finished bag can create completely different looks.

Harlequin Drum Pincushion

Pincushions date back to the 16th century and, while simple, they were an important sewing accessory for needlework and still are. They come in all shapes and sizes, from fancy Victorian-era dolls and birds to charming cushions in repurposed egg or teacups. They can be shaped like tomatoes or strawberries, be worn on the finger or wrist, and be made from all kinds of fabrics, from velvet to cotton to linen. This diamond design lets you enjoy some fun fussy cutting from your favorite scraps and is a pretty addition to any sewing space!

FINISHED PINCUSHION SIZE: 3½" x 3" (8.9cm x 7.6cm)

REQUIREMENTS

- Two fat sixteenths patterned fabrics for triangles
- Seven 4" (10.3cm) squares assorted patterned fabrics for diamonds
- Two 4½" (11.5cm) squares patterned fabrics for the top and bottom
- One 12" x 5" (30.5 x 12.8cm) rectangle lightweight iron-on fusible interfacing (I used Pellon H630)
- Coordinating cotton thread
- Templates on page 131
- Template plastic
- Fine permanent marker
- 2B pencil or ceramic lead fabric pencil
- Plastic stuffing pellets
- Polyester fiber filling

PREPARATION

Make the templates by tracing them onto the template plastic using a fine permanent marker. Cut them out on the line and label them with their numbers.

CUTTING INSTRUCTIONS

- From each of the fat sixteenths, cut:
  - Seven HD1 pieces (14 total)
- From each of the 4" (10.2cm) squares, cut:
  - One HD2 piece (7 total)
- From each of the 4½" (11.4cm) squares, cut:
  - One HD3 piece (2 total)
- From the fusible interfacing, cut:
  - One 10" x 3" (25.4 x 7.6cm) rectangle
  - Two HD3 pieces without seam allowance

CONSTRUCTION

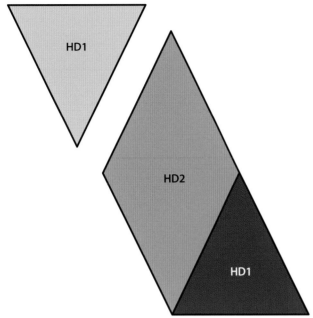

1. Stitch HD1 pieces to the top left and bottom right of an HD2 piece. Repeat to make seven units.

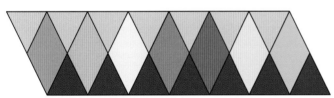

2. Stitch these units together, lining up the triangle seams. Press.

3. Iron the fusible interfacing onto the wrong side of the completed outside panel, making sure the seam allowance remains uncovered.

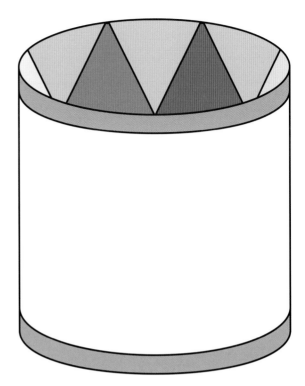

4. Stitch the panel together along the short edge to make a tube.

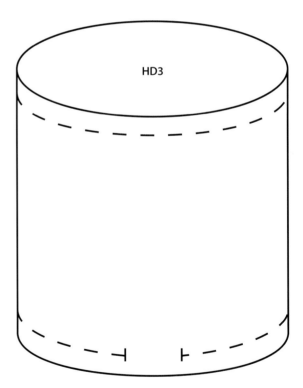

5. Iron the fusible interfacing onto the wrong side of each HD3 piece. With right sides together, stitch the HD3 circles to the top and the bottom, leaving a 1½" (3.8cm) gap in the bottom seam so you can turn the pincushion right side out and stuff it.

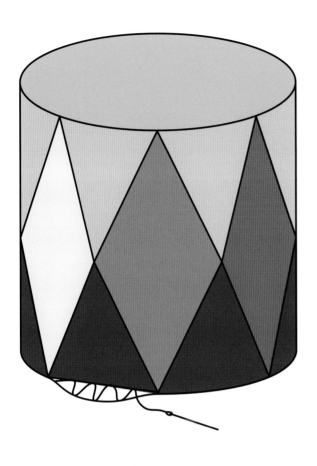

6. Stuff the pincushion and then add about ½ cup (71g) of stuffing pellets to add weight to the base. You can use a small funnel to do this neatly. Put a bit more stuffing in to keep the pellets in and then stitch the gap closed using a slip stitch.

This is another one of those scrap-busting projects that will help you use up every last bit of your favorite fabrics.

Petal Needlebook

Simple and useful additions to any sewing box, needlebooks have been around for centuries and are a perfect way to use up all the lovely scraps left over from your quilting projects. This is a fun and quick appliqué project to put together by hand or machine and would make a lovely gift for like-minded sewing friends!

FINISHED NEEDLEBOOK SIZE: 5" x 4½" (12.8 x 11.5cm)

REQUIREMENTS

- One 7" (17.8cm) square low-volume patterned fabric for front cover
- Five 3" (7.7cm) squares assorted patterned fabrics for flower appliqué
- Six 4" (10.3cm) squares assorted patterned fabrics for back cover
- Two 7" (17.8cm) squares assorted patterned fabrics for inside cover
- Fat sixteenth felted wool or wool felt for needle pages
- Fat sixteenth batting
- Size 8 perle cotton thread
- Templates on pages 132–133
- Template plastic
- Fine permanent marker
- 2B pencil or ceramic lead fabric pencil
- Coordinating cotton thread

PREPARATION

Make the templates by tracing them onto the template plastic using a fine permanent marker. Cut them out on the line and label them with their numbers.

CUTTING INSTRUCTIONS

- From the front cover fabric, cut:
  - One P1 piece
- From the flower appliqué fabrics, cut:
  - Eleven P2 pieces
  - One P3 piece

Note: Trace these onto the front of your fabric and add a generous ⅛" (3.2mm) seam allowance.

- From the back cover fabrics, cut:
  - Six P4 pieces
- From the inside cover fabrics, cut:
  - Two P1 pieces
- From the needle page fabric, cut:
  - Two P5 pieces
- From the batting, cut:
  - Two P1 pieces

CONSTRUCTION

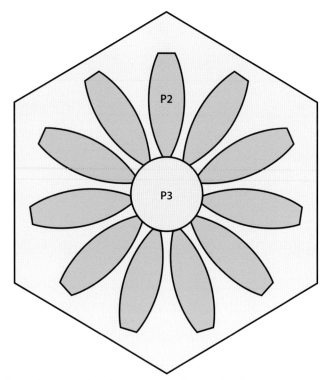

1. Following the diagram, appliqué the daisy onto the front cover, starting with the P2 petal pieces and finishing with the center P3 circle.

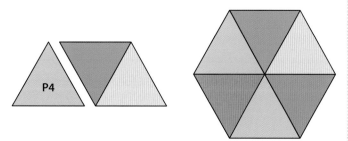

2. Stitch three P4 triangles together and repeat to make two units. Stitch these units together along the long edges to create a hexagon shape.

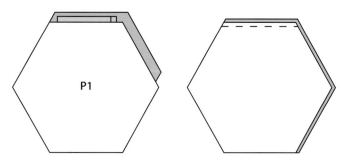

3. Take the two inside cover pieces and, with right sides together, sandwich the ¼" (6.4mm) seams of the two felt pages between, making sure the edges are even and the pages are centered. Stitch through all the layers.

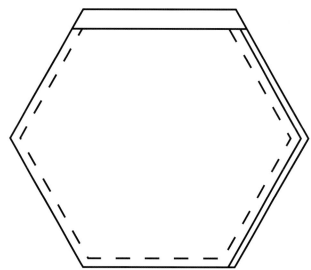

4. Baste a batting P1 piece to the wrong side of the front cover, then trim the batting away from the seam allowance on one edge. Repeat with the back cover.

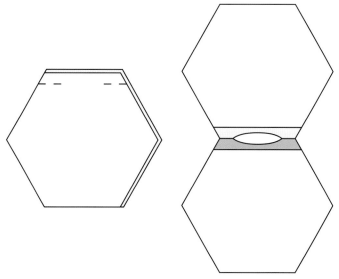

5. With right sides together, stitch the front and back cover together with a short ¾" (1.9cm) seam on either side, leaving a gap in the middle for turning the project right side out. Press the seams open.

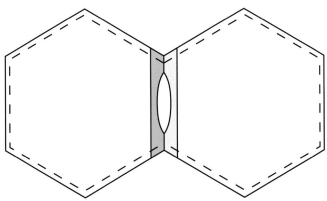

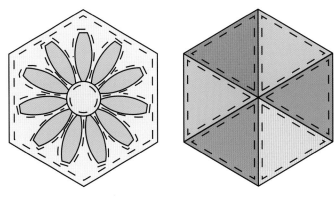

6. With right sides together, stitch the inside covers to the front and back. Keep the felt needle pages out of the way so you don't sew through them.

8. Using the perle cotton thread, stitch around the petals and center on the front cover and the triangles on the back cover using a simple running stitch. Make sure you are only stitching into the batting and not all the way through to the lining.

7. Turn the needlebook right side out and press it. Stitch the turning gap closed using a ladder stitch.

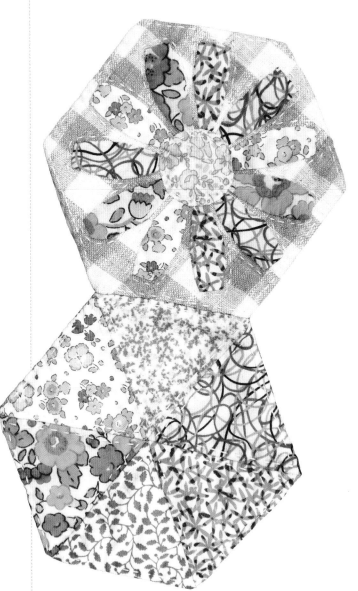

The stitching on the finished needlebook is another element that adds to the vintage charm.

Finishing Your Project

Basting, quilting, and binding with confidence takes your creativity to a new level.

Basting

The process of putting together all the layers of the quilt to prepare it for quilting is often referred to as creating the quilt sandwich. Your backing and batting need to be bigger than your quilt top as that piece can creep in during quilting. You will trim back the quilt top once it is ready to be bound. Basting can be done using curved quilting safety pins, spray glue, or large tacking stitches (thread-basting). I prefer the safety pin method described here.

1. On a large surface, such as a table or a very clean floor, lay out your quilt backing right side down. Carefully secure this to the surface using painter's tape, making sure it is smooth and taut but not tight.

2. Lay your batting on top and smooth it carefully to make sure there are no wrinkles or folds.

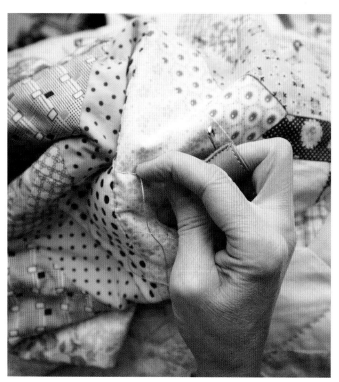

I use a leather thimble on my right middle finger to push the needle through. You will have your own pressure points, so find a comfortable and suitable thimble option to form a layer of protection while you quilt.

3. Carefully lay the quilt top right side up over the batting, making sure you leave enough backing and batting all the way around the edge of the quilt. Smooth once again, being careful not to move any of the layers.

4. Pin the layers together using curved quilting safety pins. Start pinning from the center and work outward to the edge.

Quilting

There are many ways to quilt, including machine quilting on a domestic sewing machine, professional long arm quilting on a long arm machine, or quilting by hand using a fine thread or thicker embroidery thread. I prefer to hand quilt using perle cotton thread in 8 or 12 weight as I like the look and feel it provides. You can use a quilting hoop to hold your piece while you quilt but I prefer to quilt without (also known as "lap quilting"), letting the drape and weight of the quilt provide the tension and using the following method.

1. Thread your needle and tie a single knot near the end of your thread.

2. Place your needle into your quilt top, running it between the batting and the backing and bringing the tip out where you wish to start quilting.

3. Pull the thread through to the end and then, while holding the quilt top for tension, pull gently until the knot pops through the top and settles into the batting— this is referred to as "burying the thread."

4. Place your hand that is not holding the needle under the quilt to hold the area you are working on steady. Use your middle finger to feel that the needle has come through to the back before bringing it back up to the front.

5. Using an even running stitch, make several stitches and then pull your needle through. Practice will give you more even, smaller stitches.

6. When you have finished the line of quilting, make a loop knot close to the top and put your needle back into the quilt very close to your last stitch, making sure you are between the batting and backing. Bring it up a short distance away and gently pull the thread again to bury the thread into the batting. Trim the thread.

Binding

Binding provides a clean edge to finish your pieces and is another opportunity for introducing different colors, patterns, and effects to your designs.

To bind quilts, you need to cut 2½" (6.4cm) x WOF strips. To bind pillows, you need to cut 2¼" (5.7cm) x WOF strips. Once you've cut your strips, use the following process to add the binding.

1. Join the strips together end to end with 45-degree seams, then trim the seams and press them open.

2. Press the joined binding strip in half lengthwise with the wrong sides facing.

3. Starting about halfway along one side and leaving a 6" (15.2cm) tail for joining, sew the binding to the quilt front using a ¼" (6.4mm) seam allowance.

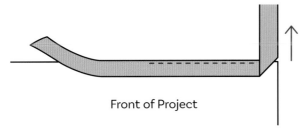

Front of Project

4. Stop ¼" (6.4mm) before you reach the first corner and backstitch to secure. Turn your quilt to prepare to sew along the next edge and take the binding up and fold it down so that the raw edge of the binding is against the quilt edge you are about to sew and the binding fold is sitting along the previously sewn edge.

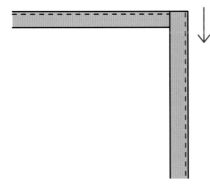

5. Start stitching again from the top edge using a ¼" (6.4mm) seam allowance.

6. Repeat steps 3 through 5 to add the binding around the entire quilt, mitering the corners. Stop about 6" (15.2cm) from the starting point.

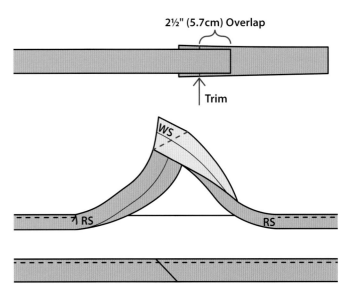

2½" (5.7cm) Overlap

Trim

WS

RS   RS

7. Overlap the two ends by 2½" (6.4cm) or the same width of the cut binding strip and join the ends with a 45-degree seam.

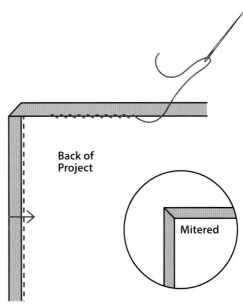

Back of Project

Mitered

8. Trim the surplus and finish sewing the binding to the quilt top. Fold the binding to the back of the quilt and slip stitch it in place along the seam line.

CUTTING FOR A BIAS BINDING

Bias binding means cutting your binding on a 45-degree angle. Some quilts require a curved binding and need the bias to be able to stretch around the curve or you might prefer the pattern on the binding to be on the bias (often for striped or check fabrics). It's also useful if you are making curved stems for appliqué designs.

1. Lay out your fabric wrong side up with the selvage to the left and right.

2. Fold the bottom left corner up to meet the top edge so that you now have a 45-degree angle (or bias edge).

3. Fold the top left corner down along the 45-degree angle so that the bias edges meet.

4. Fold it in half once again so the bias edges are on top of each other.

5. Line your ruler up with the top and bottom of the folded fabric and trim off the folded bias edges to get a straight edge.

6. Rotate the piece to the left either by picking it up or turning your cutting mat around.

7. Cut your bias binding strips.

Making a Pillow Back

This is a simple and neat way to finish your pillow back with a zipper. I like to allow a bit more backing width and then trim it back. Each pillow pattern in this book has cutting instructions for the two back pieces, and the general process is the same no matter the size.

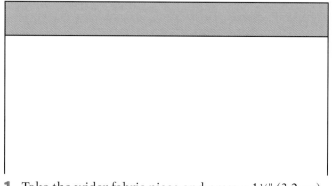

1. Take the wider fabric piece and press a 1¼" (3.2cm) fold toward the wrong side of the fabric along one long edge, making sure the fabric pattern is running in the right direction.

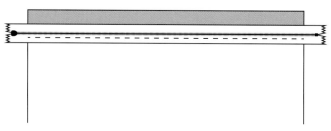

2. Place your zipper right side down and centered along the raw edge of the fold, making sure there is about ¼" (6.4mm) of the fold sitting above the top edge of the zipper. Pin and stitch along the raw edge side using a zipper foot.

The zippered pillow backing allows you to easily swap your covers with the seasons or just to change things up a bit.

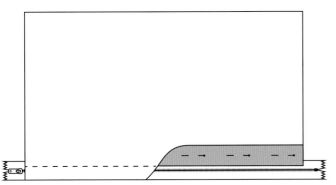

3. Turn the piece right side up and press it. The flap should now sit over the zipper. Fold the flap back up and pin it to keep it out of the way while you attach the other back section.

4. With right sides facing, pin the other side of the zipper to the long edge of the remaining back section. Stitch using the zipper foot.

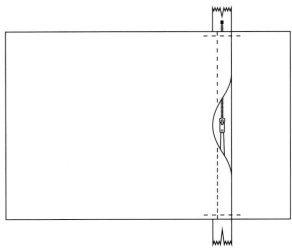

5. To prevent the zipper from coming apart when you trim off the edges, first open the zipper about halfway, then bring the top zipper edges together side by side. Lay the flap over them and pin it in place. Stitch across the pillow flap using a ⅛" (3.2mm) seam. Repeat the stitching at the other end of the zipper.

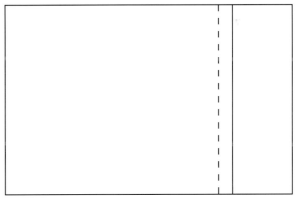

6. Trim the excess zipper off each end in line with the edges of the back. Trim the pillow back to match the pattern measurements.

Templates

Fruit Cocktail templates,
page 24

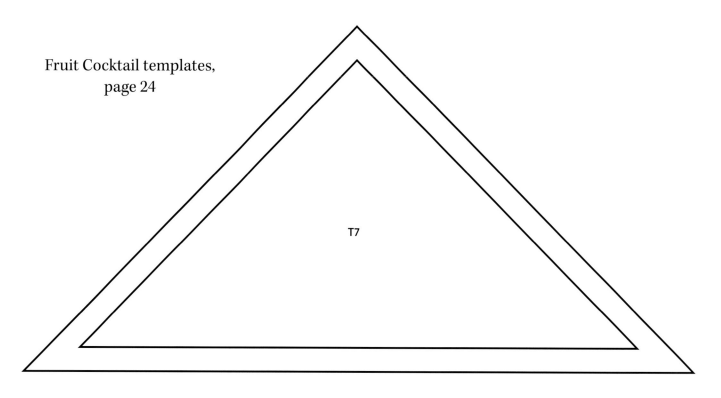

T7

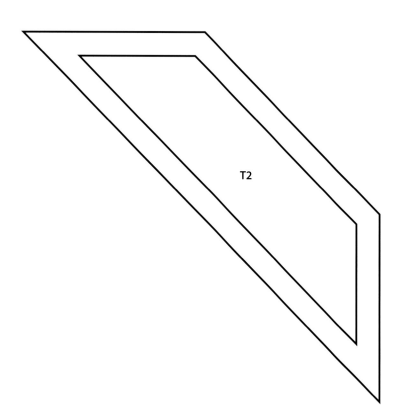

T2

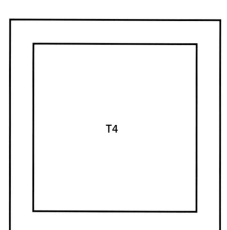

T4

T3

T1

T5

T6

Happy May Day template,
page 30

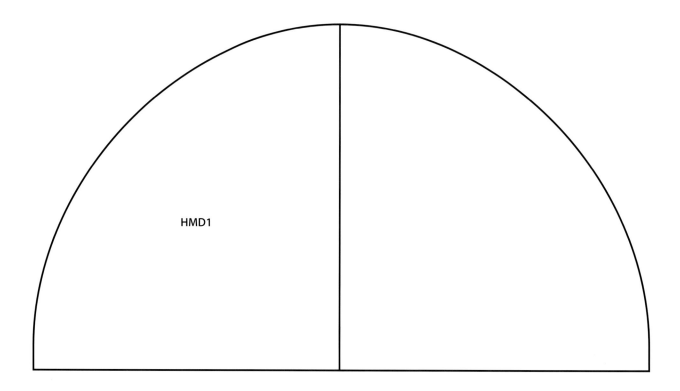

HMD1

Hyacinth template,
page 36

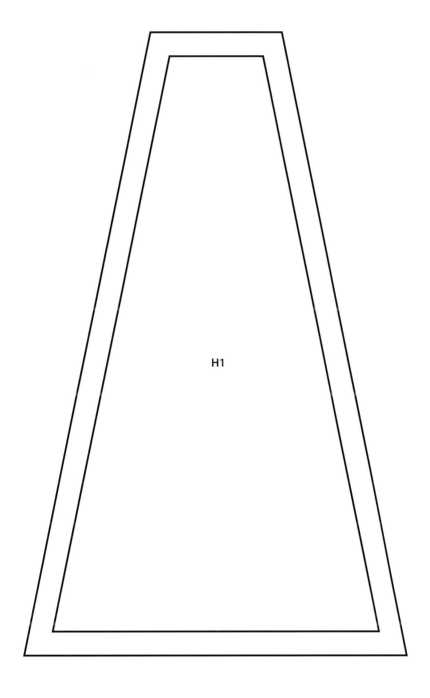

H1

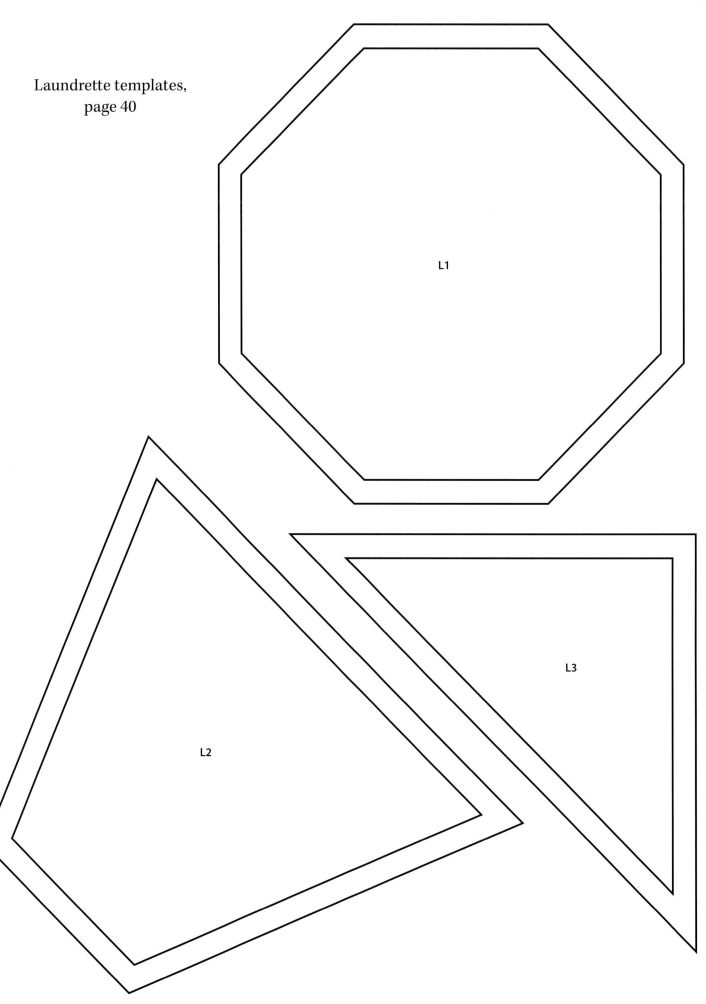

Laundrette templates,
page 40

L1

L2

L3

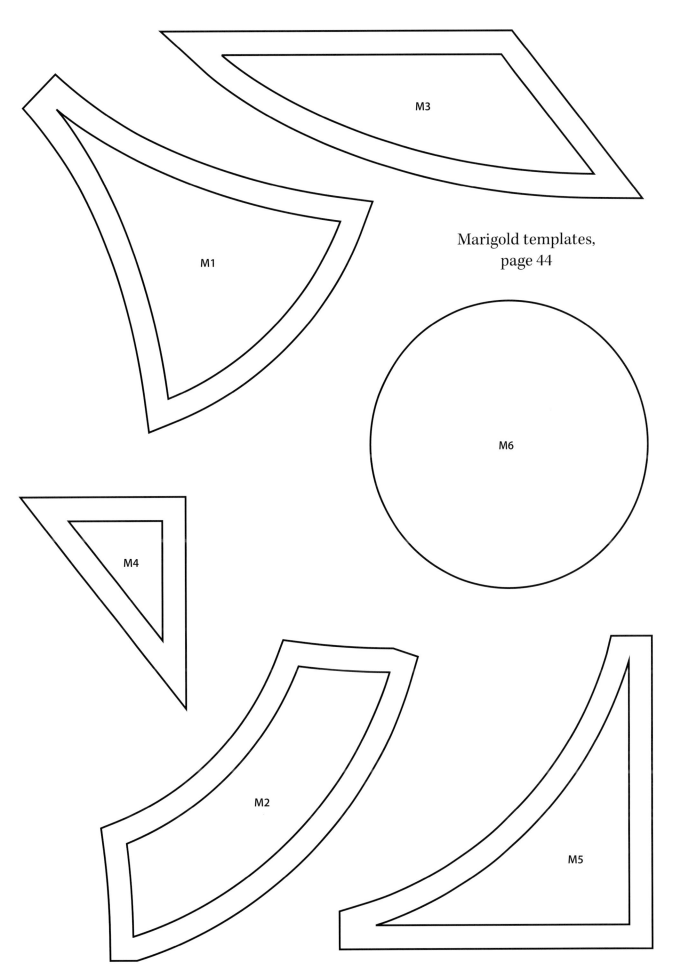

M3

M1

Marigold templates,
page 44

M6

M4

M2

M5

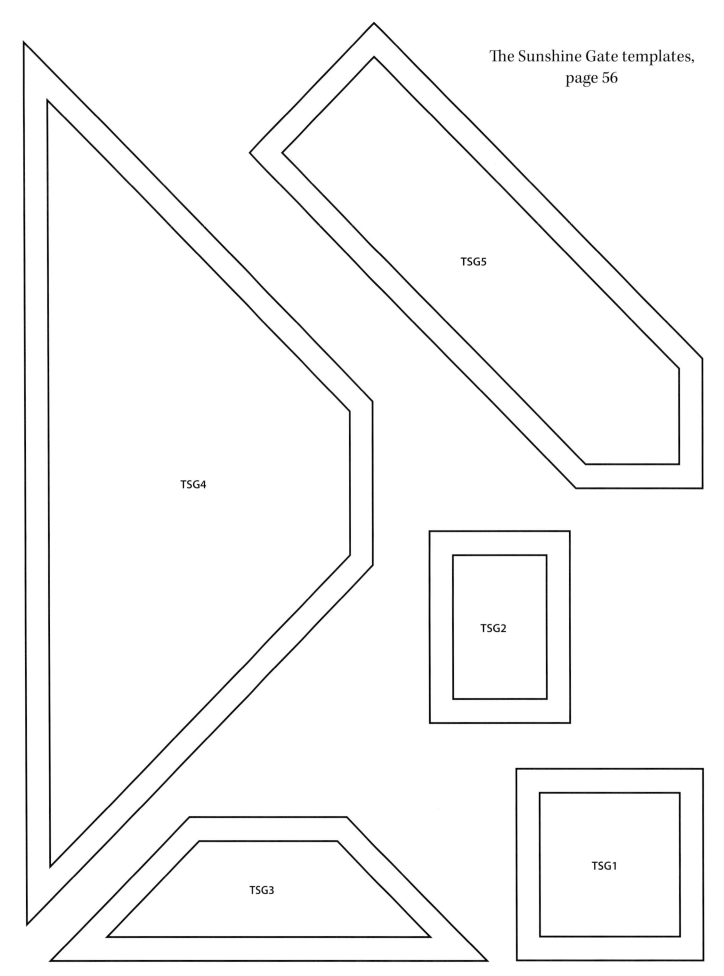

The Sunshine Gate templates,
page 56

TSG5

TSG4

TSG2

TSG1

TSG3

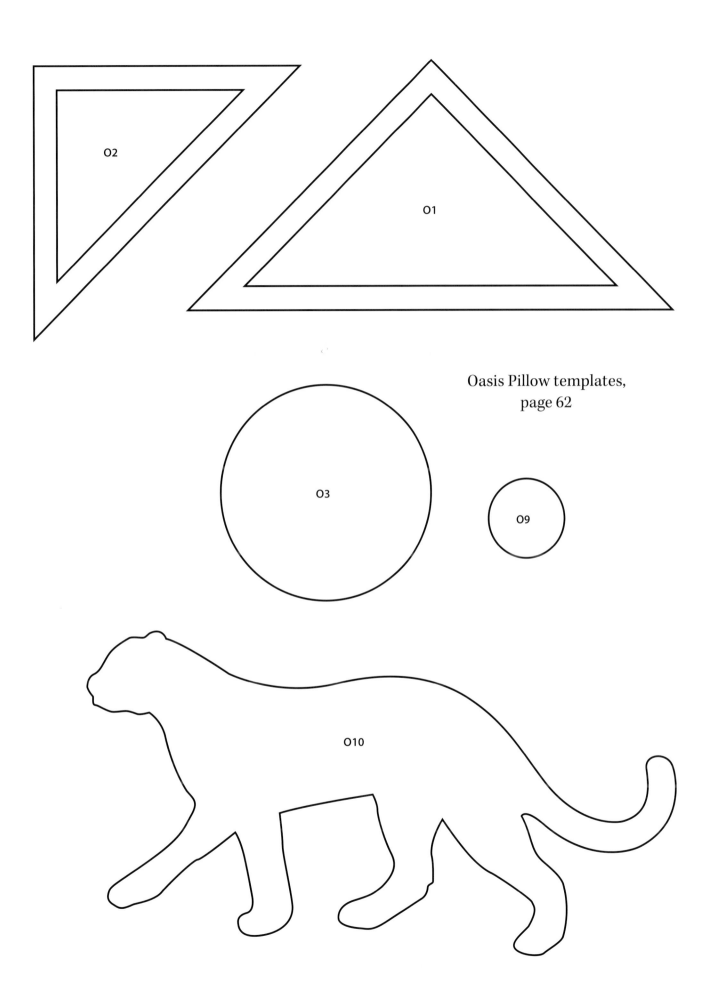

O2

O1

Oasis Pillow templates,
page 62

O3

O9

O10

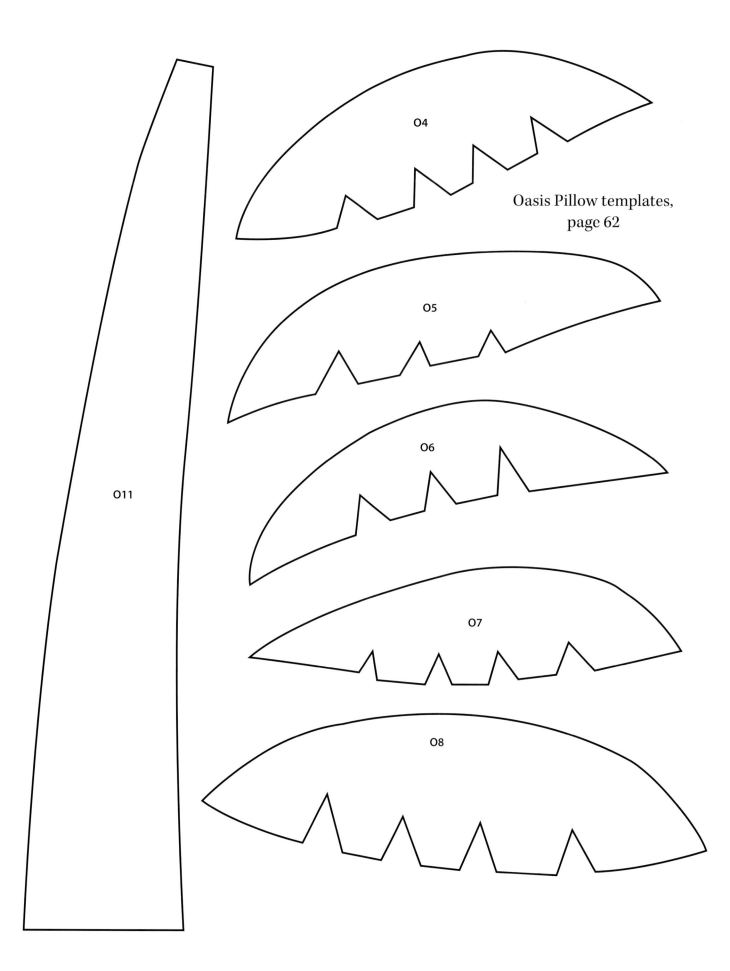

O4

O5

O6

O7

O8

O11

Oasis Pillow templates,
page 62

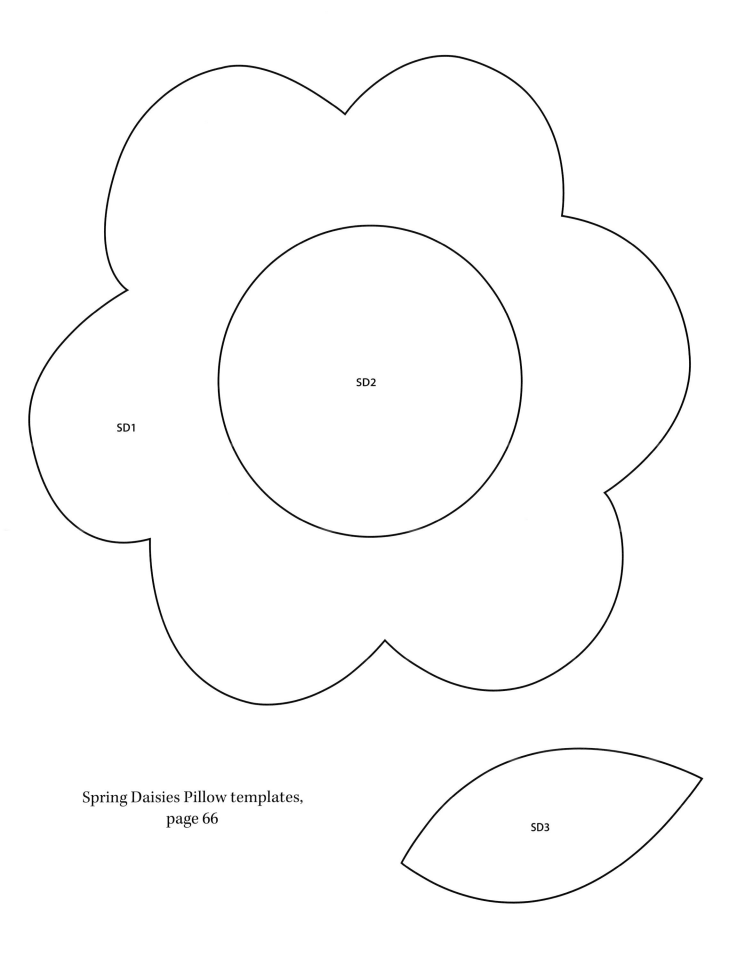

SD2

SD1

SD3

Spring Daisies Pillow templates,
page 66

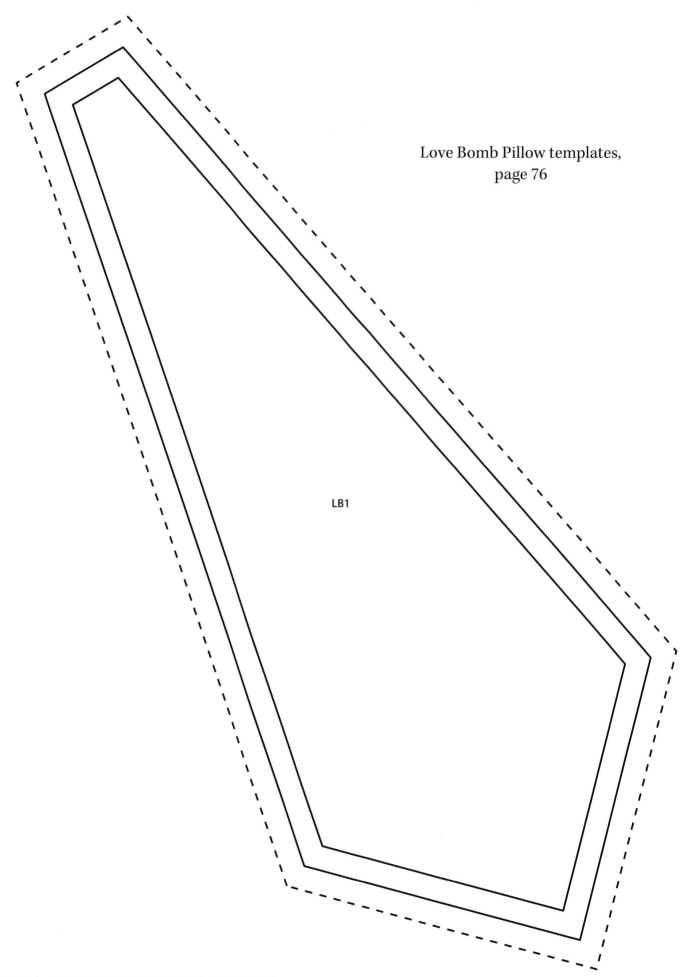

Love Bomb Pillow templates,
page 76

LB1

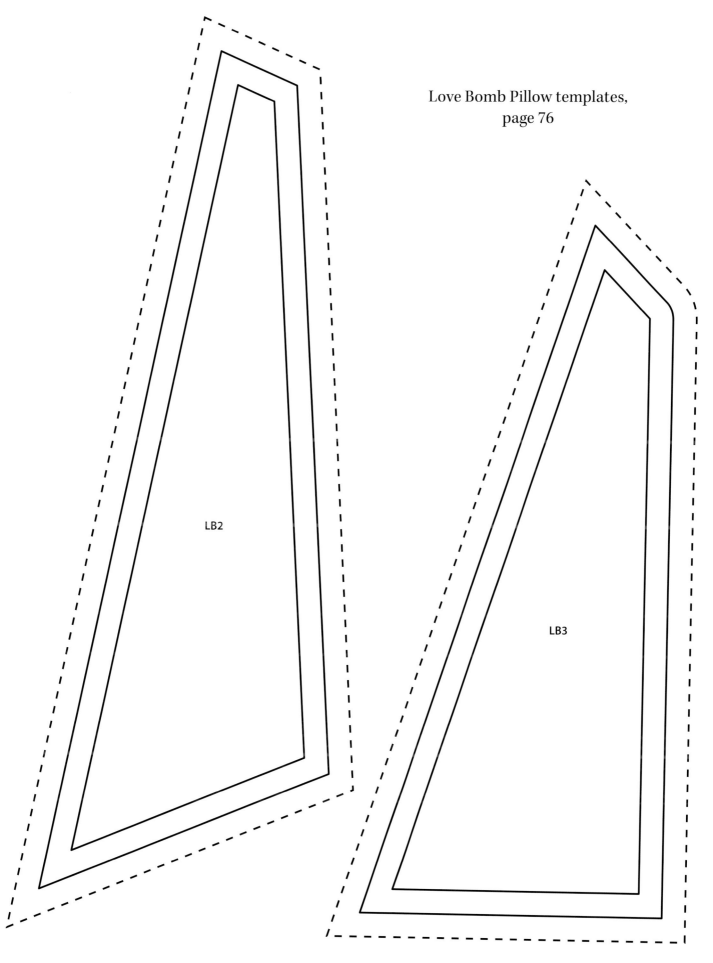

Love Bomb Pillow templates,
page 76

LB2

LB3

LB4

Love Bomb Pillow templates,
    page 76

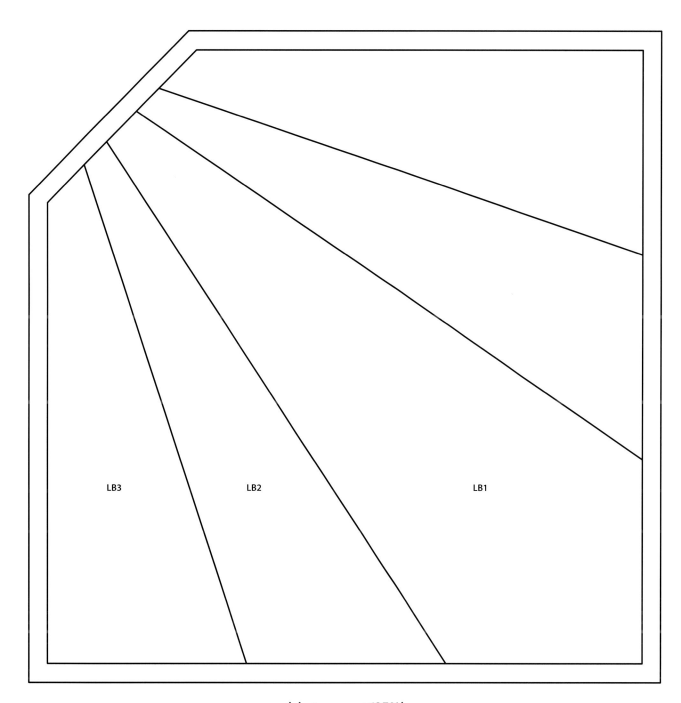

LB3   LB2   LB1

(photocopy at 125%)

Indoor Garden Pillow templates,
page 84

IG2

IG3

IG4

IG1

Plant 1

Indoor Garden Pillow templates,
page 84

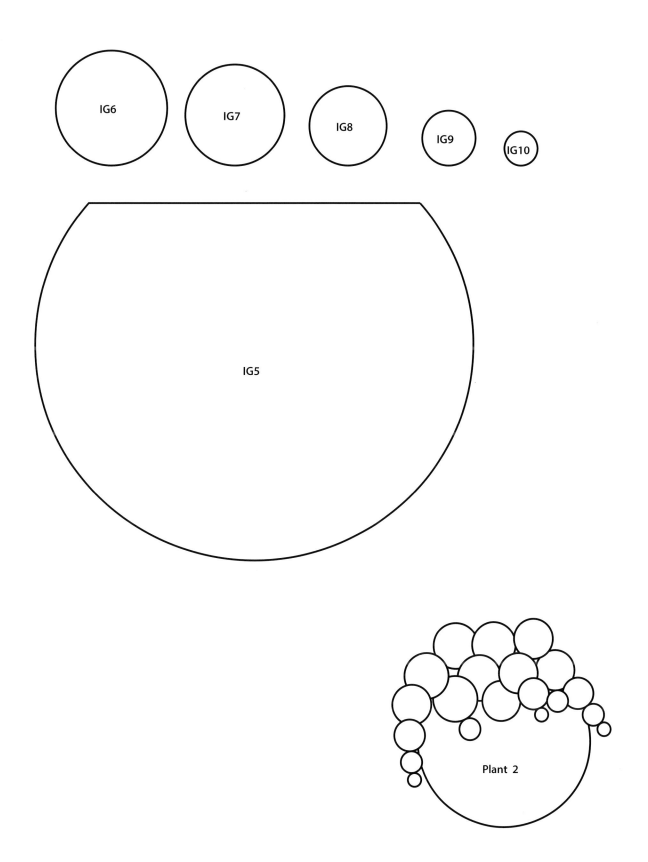

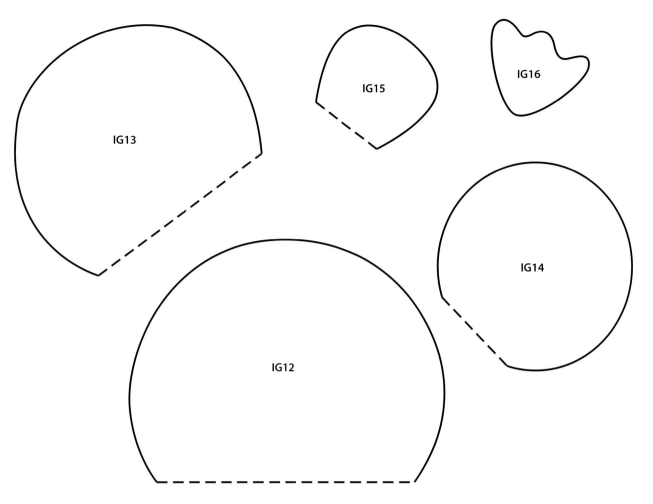

IG13

IG15

IG16

IG14

IG12

Indoor Garden Pillow templates,
page 84

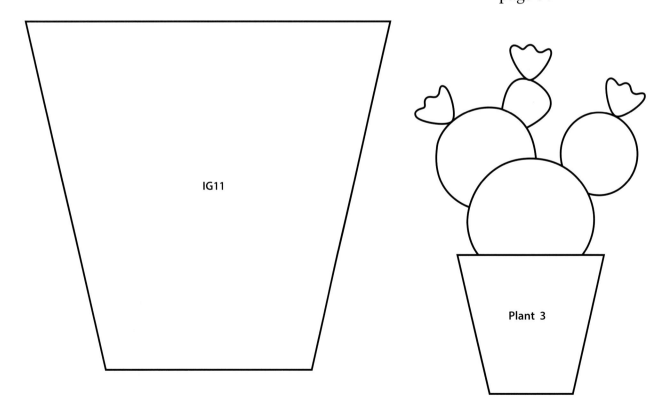

IG11

Plant 3

Indoor Garden Pillow templates,
page 84

IG20

IG21

IG22

IG19

IG17

IG18

Plant 4

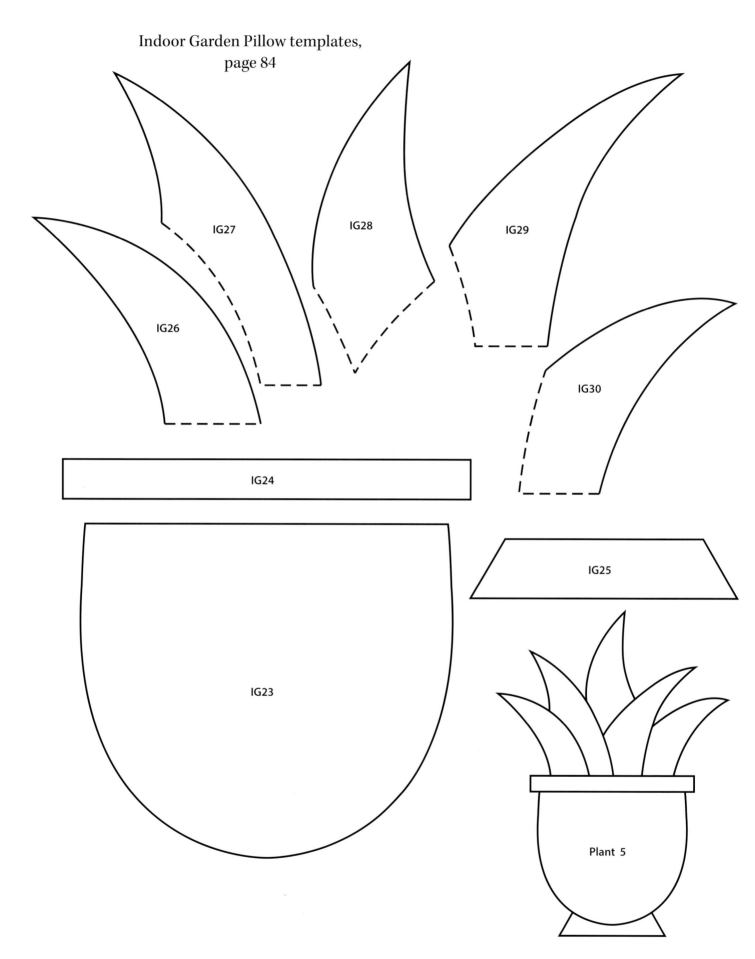

Indoor Garden Pillow templates,
page 84

IG27

IG28

IG29

IG26

IG30

IG24

IG25

IG23

Plant 5

Barley Sugar Pillow templates,
page 88

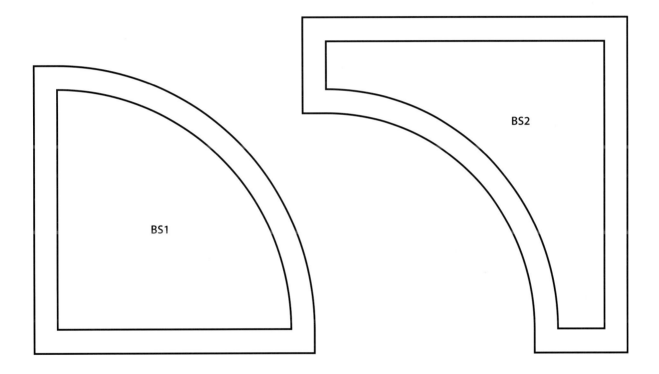

Veronica Bag templates,
page 92

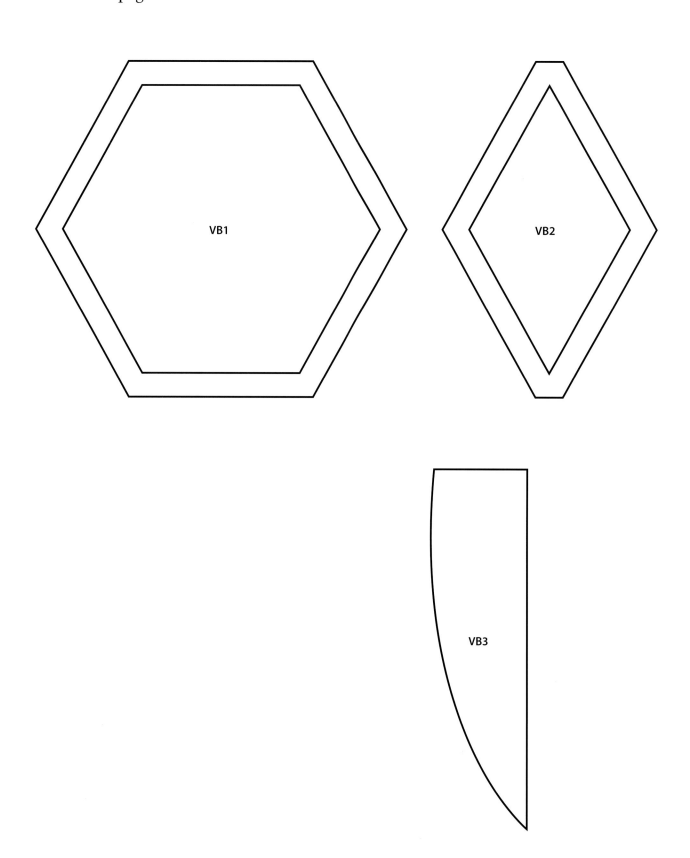

VB1

VB2

VB3

Harlequin Drum Pincushion templates,
page 98

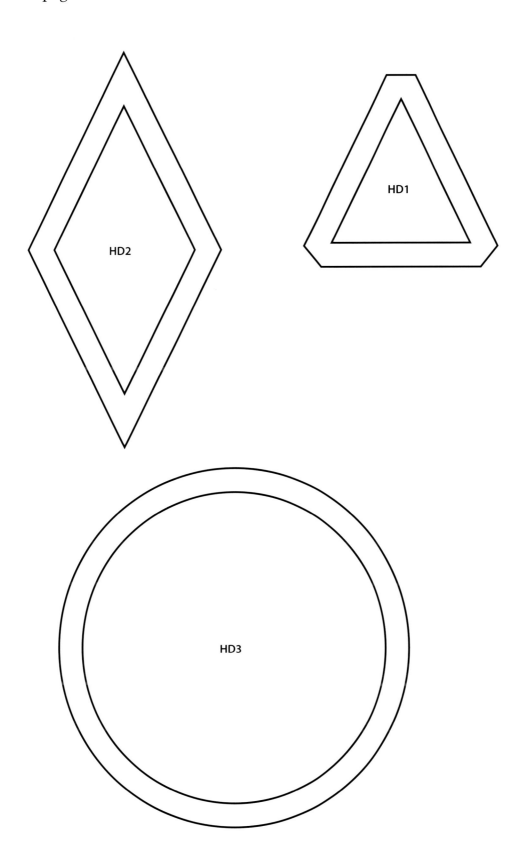

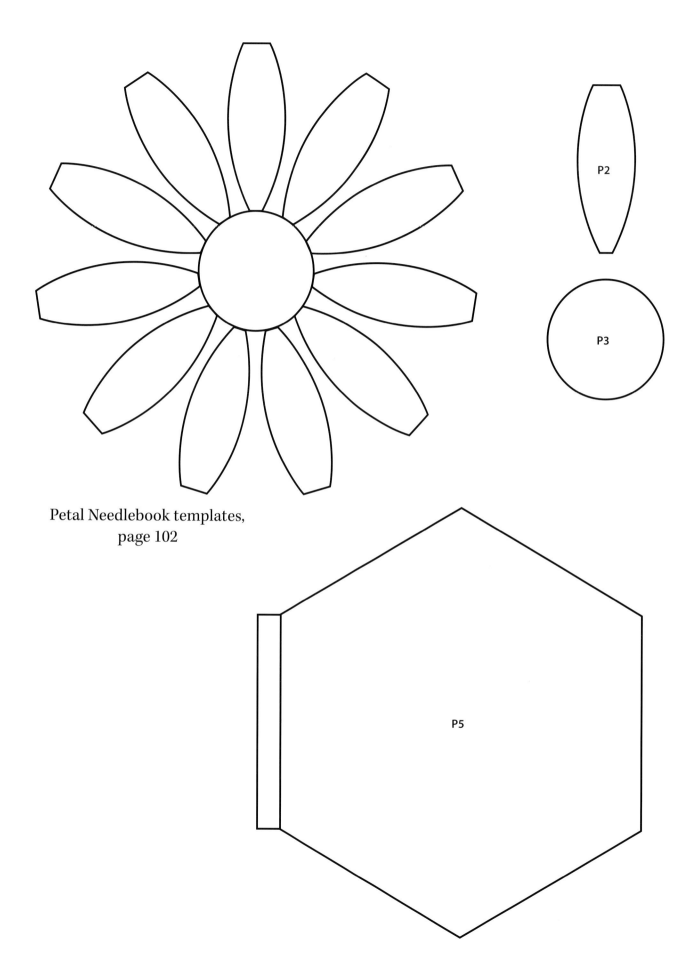

Petal Needlebook templates,
page 102

P2

P3

P5

Petal Needlebook templates,
page 102

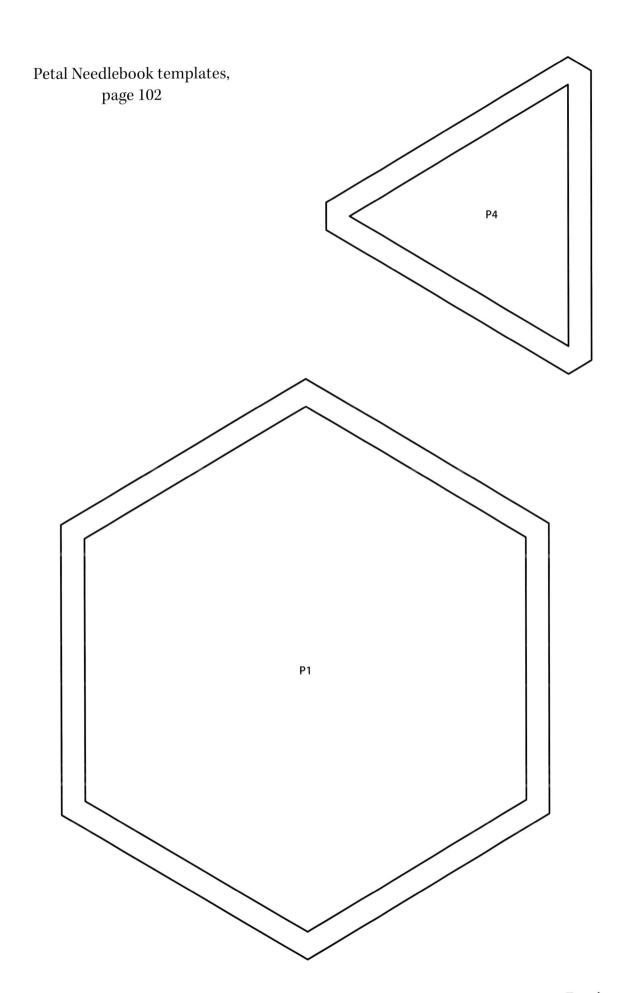

P4

P1

Index

Note: Page numbers in *italics* indicate projects and templates.

Acknowledgments

Life is so much easier when you have an amazing cheer squad behind you, and I don't know where I would be without my beautiful family! Thank you to my darling husband Bill who has patiently walked around piles of fabric and quilts for the last year as I turned our living room into a sewing studio, and who continues to provide us with delicious meals and clean washing. Thanks to my gorgeous Chloe who has turned my scribbles into perfect diagrams, brought the projects to life with her photos, and generally held my hand through this entire process. Thank you to my lovely Lucinda for being an excellent hand model for the photos, for deep cleaning nearly everything in the house and always giving me great feedback, and to my sweet Daphne—your shoulder rubs and hugs are the best and you are the expert at finding my wayward needles and pins. I'm so lucky to have their loving support and encouragement in all that I do in this quilty business!

To my dear friends Regina and Helen, thank you for your endless advice and moral support during our weekly coffee catch ups while I stitched like a crazy lady, and Christina for your wonderful photo props and many years of creative inspiration.

Special thanks to Jen Kingwell for being such a major influence and mentor in my quilting journey. From giving me the opportunity to work in your beautiful shop, Amitie Textiles, all those years ago, to inspiring me as I watched you effortlessly create beautiful fabric combinations and extraordinary quilt masterpieces. Your encouragement and advice were invaluable! And thank you to my gorgeous Amitie colleagues, Marie, Carol, Gayle, Gina, Jane, and Judy, who are each amazing quilters and have always been a great source of motivation and fun! Sorry for driving you all mad with my fabric-selecting process and constant mind changing—your opinions are always much appreciated!

I'm hugely grateful to the lovely Jemima Flendt of Tied with a Ribbon fame who, after a discussion over a quick glass of wine on one of her visits to Melbourne last year, contacted her book editor Amelia Johanson to recommend me as a suitable quilt book writer. It's supportive and generous friendships like these that make this business so wonderful! And, of course, many thanks to Amelia for being so enthusiastic about my ideas for this book and making it happen.

To all the lovely quilt shops I teach at and my fabulous students—thank you for allowing me to share my love of this wonderful craft and for your continued support of my work. I couldn't do it without you!

Finally, thank you to my beautiful Mum who taught me how to sew and gifted me with a lifelong love of creating. This book is dedicated to you.

About Louise

Louise has always had a love of making after being taught to sew, knit, and crochet by her mother. After a busy career in marketing and public relations and the birth of her three children, her love of sewing was reignited with the discovery of the online world of craft blogging. Under the pseudonym Lululollylegs, she participated in sewing swaps for pillows, bags, and doll quilts with like-minded people around the world while developing her passion for designing.

In 2007, Louise was offered a job at Jen Kingwell's Amitie Textiles, where she spent nearly ten years sharing her love of fabric and quilt making in the shop and eventually in the classroom as a teacher until the business moved to the regional coast of Victoria in 2017.

During those years, Louise released patterns under the labels Audrey and Maude and Three Dolls and has had her designs published in magazines and books in Australia, the United States, and the United Kingdom. In 2016, she was invited to design as a part of the Jen Kingwell Collective, which has taken her popular patterns, including The Avenue, Girl Next Door, and Lamingtons for Tea, worldwide.

Louise continues to be a regular teacher in Melbourne and in regional and interstate quilt stores, sharing her passion for hand piecing, quilting, and needle-turn appliqué. She has a love of vintage and scrappy quilts, art deco, and mid-century modern style, and is still inspired by beautiful fabrics every single day.

Louise lives in Melbourne, Australia, with her husband and three daughters.